All studen
or ho
can become responsible and independent learners.

"As an educator for thirty years and a proponent of higher standards, I was delighted to read this new book . . . I know that students are capable of far more than we are asking of them today. *Homework: Bridging the Gap* offers a straightforward and thoughtful program to help ensure that all students acquire the skills they need to achieve their academic goals. It links parents, students, school staff and community in a partnership that will build excellent study habits and allow young people to personalize their learning. I highly recommend this book." —TERRY BERGESON, EXECUTIVE DIRECTOR, WASHINGTON STATE COMMISSION ON STUDENT LEARNING

"*Homework: Bridging the Gap* goes far beyond providing a tidy homework system. It helps teachers, parents and students commit to putting the power of learning in the hands of the learner . . . truly a significant system and program."
—BARRY HOONAN, TEACHER AND EDUCATION CONSULTANT

"We need programs like this that build community partnerships and increase equal access to the opportunities that a good education can provide. I highly recommend this book." —RON SIMS, METROPOLITAN KING COUNTY COUNCIL MEMBER

HOMEWORK:

BRIDGING THE GAP

Kay Morison, Ph.D. & Suzanne Brady

HOMEWORK:

BRIDGING THE GAP

A GUIDE *for* BUILDING HOMEWORK PARTNERSHIPS

Kay Morison, Ph.D. & Suzanne Brady

Goodfellow Press
Redmond, WA 98053

A **Goodfellow Press**, Inc. Publication
7710 196th Avenue N.E., Redmond, WA 98043-4710

ISBN 0-9639882-5-5

Edited by Pamela R. Goodfellow
Cover and Book Design by Scott Pinzon for Pinpoint MarComm

Jennifer Maring, a sixth grade student at Emily Dickinson Elementary School, drew the illustration depicted on the cover. She lives in Redmond, Washington.

Printed and bound in the United States of America on recycled paper.

Foreword

When asked, educators and parents express the opinion that homework is necessary and valuable. However, students in the United States aren't spending much time doing it, especially when compared to students in other countries. Parents, teachers, and students have strong, and often differing, opinions about the amount and type of assignments that should serve as homework. The lack of information about homework and the difficulty of maintaining communication between schools and parents about daily schoolwork have hindered our ability to create effective homework systems. A homework partnership that bridges the communication gap between school and home can help students acquire the skills they need to face academic tasks with confidence.

International comparisons illustrate that American students lag far behind their counterparts in other countries, especially in science and math. However, improved scores and better grades are not the goal of reform, they are a by-product. The goal of reform is to enable all students to develop their talents to the best of their ability so that they can lead satisfying and productive lives. In order to take advantage of opportunities in our increasingly technological world, students need to be academically competent. For measurable change in achievement to occur, it is important to give our students the tools they need so that they are able to persist in the face of difficulty. These techniques include the ability to communicate ideas effectively, to retrieve information efficiently, and to acquire problem solving skills that they can apply to many tasks. Equally important is a positive attitude toward learning. Students who view mistakes as valuable sources of information, rather than as threats to self-esteem or signs of failure, learn how to persevere. A homework system based on time spent in study can foster a positive attitude toward challenging academic tasks. When students learn how to study, spend sufficient time doing worthwhile homework, and are given encouragement to follow the dictates of their interests and curiosity, they take the first step toward becoming lifelong learners.

A homework system that encourages rigorous academic pursuit and, at the same time, respects individual differences is imperative. What is needed is a homework system that rewards effort and initiative rather than competition. All students, regardless of ability level and home circumstances, can become responsible and independent learners. Students can learn how to make choices that best suit their individual talents and goals. This can be accomplished without asking teachers to prescribe individual assignments.

The basic building blocks of reform are accurate information and specific solutions that can be tailored to the needs of diverse communities. The proposed homework system was developed by an experienced teacher. The Brady System is simple to implement, yet based on profound underlying principles. An experienced teacher refined the system during her twenty-three years of teaching in public schools. The homework research was compiled and summarized by an educational psychologist and researcher who has worked with students at all levels, from kindergarten through adult education. This book is a result of their collaboration.

- What is the Brady homework system?
- What does research have to say about homework?
- Is the Brady System based on sound learning theory and practice?
- Are student motivation and responsibility enhanced by a school-wide homework system?
- What are the essential qualities of any effective homework system?

The research summary included in the text enables teachers and community members to judge the effectiveness of any proposed homework solution. All changes in our system of education should be accompanied by clear explanations and references from research. Background material should be readily available to those who will be affected by decisions. Shared information is the key to developing partnerships. Informed communities are more likely to step out of the cycle of blame and to become involved in supporting school activities. Procedures for gathering community input and implementing school-wide homework systems are included in this book. When solutions are generated and adopted by the people who will be affected by decisions, the result is greater cooperation.

The proposed homework system addresses the needs of all persons involved in the education of our children. Mutual respect is the groundwork for the partnership. The system protects teacher autonomy and professionalism. At the same time, it encourages parent participation and student interests. It is a flexible system, simple to implement and monitor, yet can have a profound and positive effect on our students' study habits.

Parents who participate in this homework system find that their children are completing their homework with increasingly less supervision. These same parents report a greater understanding of classroom activities. Teachers note the positive effect of extended study time taking place outside the classroom walls. Student effort and enthusiasm increase dramatically. Students who have often accepted "I can't" as their motto begin to say, "I can." At the same time, parents who struggle with busy schedules and who already devote time helping their children with homework appreciate the simplicity that this homework system brings to their daily routine. Homework completion is ultimately the student's responsibility, but motivation can be enhanced through a working partnership between the home and the school.

ACKNOWLEDGMENTS

The information supplied by Sandy Troudt, an educator and administrator at Charlie Lake Elementary School, B.C. is gratefully acknowledged. Thanks are also due to Sally Astridge, Margit Moore, Cindy Wykoff, Sharon Plowman, May Thompson, and Dawn Todd for their hours of editing, and to Scott Pinzon for the design of the book. The efforts of Barbara Woolsey, a dedicated Carl Sandburg teacher, and Chris Larson, the chairman of the Carl Sandburg Homework Committee were invaluable. They facilitated parent-staff communication about homework with unfailing good humor and professionalism.

The collective wisdom and individual insights of the members of the Carl Sandburg Homework Committee were the inspiration for the completion of the project. The Homework Committee provided a model of parent-teacher collaboration. Members tackled a controversial subject by gathering information, engaging in open, positive discussion, and formally soliciting parent, student and staff input. The committee shared consensual solutions with the entire community and provided for ongoing evaluation. These "school people" make the partnership work. Finally, the encouragement and support of Pamela R. Goodfellow helped our vision become a reality.

Table of Contents

The Brady System

"Since using this approach, more students do more homework of a purposeful nature than I've ever had before; more books read, more writing, more math at higher levels of thinking, more creative and thoughtful use of their time."
— Suzanne Brady

CHAPTER 1

THE NEED FOR CHANGE

There is a great deal of public concern over the current state of American education. Too many of our children are failing to meet their potential. The perception exists that problems in education are confined largely to children at risk of school failure but there is also mounting evidence that gifted and talented students are not thriving under current conditions.

Over a decade ago, the National Commission on Excellence in Education found that American student achievement was far surpassed by their counterparts in other countries. The report was entitled appropriately, "A Nation At Risk." More recent studies have confirmed the commission's findings, particularly in science and math (Stevenson, Chen, Lee, 1992; Walberg, et al, 1985). Despite a decade of public focus on school reform, comparison of the performance of elementary and secondary school students between 1980 and 1990 reveals a decline from first through eleventh grade in the relative position of American students in mathematics and science. Test scores are one indicator that changes need to be made. They do not reveal the entire picture. Students from all ethnic and cultural backgrounds are capable of high achievement. United States students face social pressures that sometimes compete with schooling. Our students watch more television, date more often, and take on after school jobs at an earlier age than students from other countries. Students are bombarded with commercial and social stimulation from an early age onward. This stimulation can have positive effects, however, educational priorities sometimes take a back seat.

> "The United States is squandering one of its most precious resources—the gifts, talents, and interests of many of its students. In a broad range of intellectual and artistic endeavors, these youngsters are not challenged to do their best work. This problem is especially severe among economically disadvantaged and minority students, who have access to fewer advanced educational opportunities and whose talents often go unnoticed."
> —OFFICE OF EDUCATIONAL RESEARCH AND IMPROVEMENT, UNITED STATES DEPARTMENT OF EDUCATION, 1994

A number of indicators point to the need to change the way we educate our students. For example, compared with students in other industrialized countries, American students are offered a less rigorous curriculum. They also read fewer demanding books, do less homework, and enter the work force less prepared. The talents of minority children have been especially neglected. Almost one in four American children lives in poverty, representing an enormous pool of untapped talent. Yet most programs focus on solving the problems they bring to school, rather than challenging them to develop their strengths.

The performance of low-income children shows a marked decline in the middle grades. The reason is not due to differences in innate ability (Chall, et al., 1990). Many of these children spend less time doing homework in the early grades. The effect of less exposure to academic activities becomes noticeable during the middle grades as they begin to experience less success and to fall behind their peers in achievement. The decrease in time spent doing homework makes a greater difference as students progress through the school system. In order to bridge the "exposure gap" and to give all of our students the opportunity to develop their unique talents to the fullest, a homework partnership that applies to all students is a necessity.

Improving the chances of success for students who are discouraged does not mean lowering standards nor simplifying curriculum. It does mean that we need to increase opportunities for these students to master the processes involved in achievement. One of the most important of these processes is time spent in study (Keith et al., 1986). Time spent doing homework is one of the most powerful predictors of achievement uncovered in education research.

Another key success factor is the student's own view

of intelligence. Some children view intelligence as something that is activated by effort. They believe that a person gets smarter by trying hard. These children often respond to difficult tasks by planning strategies to overcome failure. In their words, they try harder and practice more. Their strategies improve with practice, and they are increasingly able to deal with the demands of more difficult projects.

Other children develop a belief that a person is born with a certain amount of ability that determines how smart they are (Henderson & Dweck, 1990). These children are more likely to lose confidence in themselves when faced with tasks that are difficult. They are also apt to reject the chance to learn something new if it involves the risk of error or confusion. This view of ability can be changed. Children can be taught to see mistakes as valuable guides for future effort. More effective attitudes can be fostered by homework practices that do not penalize students for making mistakes. A system that gives credit for time spent in study encourages students to view mistakes as sources of information, not evidence of lesser ability. The goal is to increase opportunities for practice and exploration and to teach students to persevere.

The Brady Homework System is designed to ensure that students from all ethnic groups and income levels are among our top performers. It is also designed to encourage children to be independent and to make choices that fit their individual talents. The goal is to enable students to make responsible decisions, rather than become trapped on a path that stifles their potential. It is not enough for teachers and parents to work in isolation toward this goal. Homework partnerships between families and schools can support learning and self-esteem. This can be accomplished without an additional burden to our teachers' daily workload or emptying the taxpayers' pocket.

Several recent surveys reflect student, parent and teacher concern with this issue, yet many school districts in the United States lack school-wide homework policies (Turvey, 1986). When policies are stated they usually include a description of desired goals such as: students will work independently on homework, students will complete homework on time, students will use handwriting guidelines and standard format. Some school handbooks also include homework time guidelines and suggested activities. What is typically left out is the daily process through which our children learn to complete homework independently and to produce quality work.

The homework system proposed in this book uses a step-by-step process to support the development of study habits and independence. Most experts recommend that schools communicate their homework policy in detail to parents. Until now, the connection has not been made between homework partnerships and the development of skills and self-esteem. It is not enough to determine what end results are desirable. It is necessary to develop means to achieve those ends.

Even though students in the United States spend less

time on homework than students in other countries, they experience more stress and academic anxiety than their counterparts in Japan and China (Stevenson, Chen, and Lee, 1992). Many students have not developed the study skills needed to cope with the learning requirements of an increasingly complex world, nor do they have the self-confidence needed to take on academic challenges. Stress results from feelings of incompetence and lack of control. We need to help students take control of their daily lives. A routine, long-range homework system can reduce the anxiety.

The first step toward positive change is information. True educational reform requires the knowledgeable participation of all parties; parents, teachers, and students. It is a myth that low-income and minority parents are indifferent toward their children's education. Research on attitudes toward school indicate that most parents have a strong commitment to their children's education and are willing to take a more active role (Chavkin, 1989). However, many families, regardless of economic status do not know what steps to take.

Homework is the perfect place to begin. Several school communities have found that the process of discussing homework issues is also an effective way to build permanent information networks at individual school sites. A homework system can bridge the communication gap between classrooms and families.

Chapter Two explains how the Brady System works, what is expected of students, teachers and parents, and what students' new homework schedules might look like. The method is simple to implement but it is based on sound principals. This homework policy can be of enormous benefit to our students.

CHAPTER 2

SUPPLYING THE SCAFFOLD

Higher achievement is the by-product of the Brady System. We know the system is working when we see students tackle difficult academic tasks willingly and persevere when they meet obstacles. The psychological outcome is a lifelong passion for learning.

What is the goal underlying this homework system?

The goal of the Brady System is to enable students to become independent learners. The outcome is to increase time spent in meaningful learning activities. These activities may be teacher-assigned or independently chosen by the student.

Students are responsible for their own learning and for making decisions that enhance their unique abilities. A step-by-step daily routine can show them how to develop greater responsibility and independence.

Parents and guardians* can help their children develop study habits, motivation, and self-esteem. They support their children's achievement by encouraging study time.

---

* The use of the word "parent" implies primary care giver.

Teachers have the means to help build a culture which supports and values learning. Students can begin to achieve their academic goals, regardless of social or economic background. Teachers can assist families with a daily process for enhancing study habits.

What is the underlying learning model?

The Brady Homework System encompasses two distinct views of students and their role in the learning process. One is the model of "student as apprentice" in which students learn the tools of the trade from experts in the field. Among the tools that the student acquires through practice are: verbal and written communication skills, logical thinking, and problem solving techniques. Teachers take a direct role in guiding the acquisition of these skills. Parents play an active roll by encouraging sufficient time for study. The Brady Homework System sets up a scaffold by requiring the effort and time on task that all apprentices need to master fundamental skills.

Perseverance is rewarded in the form of full credit for homework time regardless of the outcome of a student's work. The Brady System rewards effort even if a project is less than perfect. However, the system does encourage rigor. Students will be given feedback on most of the projects they undertake. Homework will be evaluated according to established classroom practice. Students are held accountable for time and for completion.

Students acquire skill faster and more efficiently when they view mistakes as valuable information about what to do next. Students who are afraid to take risks are trapped by their lack of self-confidence. In general, setting lower standards will not benefit our students. Rather, assigning meaningful tasks and not penalizing them for mistakes will encourage their efforts.

Several researchers have studied the characteristics of highly creative and productive people. Vera John Steiner (1985) described the experiences of scientists and artists in their process of moving from apprentice to expert. A well-known biologist described how she became skilled in her field:

> "Above all, there is freedom, the knowledge that you were going to make mistakes and not being afraid. To be frightened . . . is to be in prison. By the end of that time I was dropping mistakes right, left, and center. I learned to love making mistakes."
>
> —A. BRITO, IN JOHN-STEINER, 1985, P. 180

The second learning model embodied in the Brady System is the student as explorer, following a path guided by his or her own curiosity and desire to know. Several studies of high achievers in both the sciences and the arts emphasize the importance of opportunities to participate in independent explorations and discovery. The system encourages students to develop their interests by insisting upon some student choice activities guided by teachers and parents.

One of many advantages of the Brady System is respect for the student as apprentice and for the student as explorer. Both student roles are important. Teacher-assigned homework is meaningful according to the teacher's professional judgment. Self-choice work reflects the students' and their caregivers' values.

What behaviors are required?

In some form or another, all school districts ask that teachers assign meaningful work, that students complete homework assignments, and parents provide an environment conducive to study. However, the Brady System adds new objectives for students and parents so that students are accomplishing homework goals.

Students will complete homework assignments outside of the classroom by:

- Setting aside enough time to meet minimum time requirements.
- Recording each week, in writing, the amount of time spent on required assignments and on independently chosen projects.
- Making independent homework choices that enhance understanding of academic topics and/or individual interests.

Parents will provide an environment conducive to the development of effective study habits by:

- Signing the weekly homework calendar indicating their awareness of teacher-assigned homework and student-chosen projects, and validating the indicated minutes spent on homework.

- Supporting their child's classroom minimum time requirements for study.
- Providing a television-free workplace for studying.
- Supplying help when needed and praise and encouragement for effort.

Teachers will encourage the development of independent study habits by:

- Setting minimum weekly time requirements for homework.
- Providing feedback for teacher-assigned work.
- Requiring independent homework choices.
- Establishing a routine time for submitting homework logs.
- Communicating with students and parents regarding homework policies.

The behaviors outlined above will help accomplish the overall objective. Students will study enough to develop skill and self-confidence.

The Brady System is simple, easy to administer and straightforward. The basic procedure can be described in a sample classroom letter for parents, a few capsule comments, and an example of a homework schedule.

What might a sample letter say?

Dear Parents,

Today your child is bringing home the homework schedule we will use throughout the school year. This schedule reflects study habits emphasized in our classroom. Your child's basic responsibility will be to bring it home on Monday, fill in the schedule with work completed and time spent and return it on Friday.

Your child will always have ____* minutes of homework each evening. I find that most students do much more than that. Since using this approach, students do more homework of a purposeful nature than ever before: more books read, more writing, more math at higher levels of thinking, more creative and thoughtful use of their time.

I will assign required homework each week. There will be class assignments and sometimes individual assignments. Most students finish these before the middle of the week and are left with time they owe me. They must decide how to spend that time. The ultimate responsibility is to their own emerging awareness of themselves as scholars.

I always make suggestions for extra things to do. Some will use these suggestions, others will pursue their own paths of interest. For example: a child may choose to write letters, finish a story, complete an art project, design a science experiment, practice handwriting, learn the multiplication tables, or build a rocket.

---

* Amount of homework time required will vary with grade level and the requirements of your school district.

Reading is a high priority activity for extra time. Students may choose their own themes, authors and genres. The title of the book, pages read, and time spent reading must be indicated on the schedule, not just "Read for sixty minutes."

I have included a space on the schedule for parents to sign and make comments. Please use that space for communication about your scholar's progress or suggestions for me to consider. I do ask that you sign the schedule after it has been completed. This homework system should help make work at home more rewarding.

Sincerely,

(Your Child's Teacher)

Capsule Comments (K–6th grade):

1. Homework envelopes go home on Monday (or the first school day of the week).
2. Required homework is listed on the schedule.
3. Students are to spend a minimum of ________ minutes a day or ________hours per week on homework.
4. Work completed and time spent are to be filled in daily in the space provided on the schedule. To indicate reading as homework, indicate the title and number of pages read.
5. Parents, please sign the schedule before homework is returned.

6. Envelope with completed homework (neatly done) is due on Friday or the last day of the school week.
7. Homework will be evaluated by the classroom teacher on the front of the envelope using one of the following symbols:

   - Required homework was not completed and/or minimum time not met

   + Required hours used and homework satisfactory

   ++Additional time spent and work well done

8. Homework will be further assessed with a quarterly grade on the report card based on predetermined requirements. If the evaluation system explained above is used, teachers can tell students exactly how many + 's are required for an honors homework grade. Students can choose to work for the desired grade. All students can excel in a homework system based on "time." Note: Some school districts will choose to evaluate homework with anecdotal remarks based on teacher input and student self-evaluation rather than grades.

What are the minimum required study times?

These time guidelines are based on the research. It is important to remember that these requirements are minimum study times. When students understand the reason for practice or if they are interested in their assignments, they generally choose to spend far more time in study and exploration.

Kindergarten	15 min.	5th grade	50 min.
1st grade	20 min.	6th grade	60 min.
2nd grade	25 min.	7th grade	80 min.
3rd grade	30 min.	8th grade	90-120 min.
4th grade	45 min.		

After reviewing the research on homework, Charlie Lake Elementary School in British Columbia decided to use the following daily minimums for their trial use of the Brady System:

Entry Level	10 minutes per night (reading to your child or talking about his/her experiences)
Primary 2	10-15 minutes daily
Primary 3	15-20 minutes daily
Primary 4	20-25 minutes daily
Intermediate 1	20-30 minutes daily'
Intermediate 2	30-40 minutes daily
Intermediate 3	40-60 minutes daily
Intermediate 4	45-60 minutes daily

Students, parents and teachers who have used the system have the following to say about the amount of time spent completing homework.

> "I am pleased with the fact that after we do what we are assigned, we make up our own homework, it's more fun than just doing assigned stuff.

I have never done homework this way and I am enjoying it. I think this homework system is very good because you have to think everyday for about 45 minutes and that warms up your brain. But why 45 minutes? Why not 100 minutes? That would get a kid going. I think it is a good idea to give some homework and let the kids find something to do for the rest of the week." — GINGER GUZMAN, FIFTH GRADE STUDENT

"My students are going way over the required study times. Once they get going on a book or a project they don't want to stop." —BARBARA NUNN, SIXTH GRADE TEACHER

"I don't know what sort of feedback you have been receiving regarding our new homework policy, but I love it! I find that my daughter now spends more time doing learning activities instead of pondering what's on television. On her own, she's doing more science experiments, math, reading, writing in her journal and simply playing, which is quite creative in and of itself.

"What I like the most is not even what she's learning with the extra studying time, but that she's getting into the great habit of just knowing on her own that it has to be done! This has to prove helpful for her as she gets into the upper grades of school. I also like the flexibility of the program. Due to the limited assigned homework, my daughter has a lot of freedom to choose what she wants to do on any given day." —DEBBIE SANDONA, PARENT OF A THIRD GRADE STUDENT

The next page shows a sample of a weekly Homework Schedule. Teachers will modify the schedule to fit their routine and preferences. From kindergarten through sixth grade it is important to set up a weekly routine means of communicating with parents about homework requirements which also requires student recording of time spent in homework and type of homework activity.

Homework Log

_______ Grade _________ min. per day

Required Homework: (Teacher assigned)

Monday:

Tuesday:

Wednesday:

Thursday:

Student Signature ________________ Total time _______

Parent Signature ________________________________

Comments:

Chapter 3
Advantages of the Brady Homework System

The homework system promotes individualization. Students who need extra practice in a particular academic area may use all of their homework time completing an assignment. The record of time spent on a particular type of assignment alerts teachers and parents to those students who may need extra help. Because the homework log is a weekly record, less time is lost before a child receives help. The routine nature of the homework log allows teachers and parents to communicate efficiently. At a glance parents can see what activities are required and how their child is using study time. The most important advantage of a time-based system is that students become less discouraged. They are given credit for effort even if they are not able to master the assignment. Thus, they are encouraged to practice.

This system benefits students who are particularly capable. Students who finish work quickly may choose to move ahead in math, explore history in greater depth, or pursue other academic interests. They receive encouragement in the form of time credit for moving ahead independently.

This system encourages responsibility. It promotes student independence by requiring students to make choices and allocate their time.

> "You can really see an improvement in my students' work. I teach primary grade students and this is really building habits!" —CARLA VENNIS, TEACHER, CHARLIE LAKE ELEMENTARY SCHOOL, B.C., CANADA

Homework becomes just that, a habit, because the system is long-range (kindergarten through sixth grade), developmental (time requirements increase with age) and it provides accountability. Students are responsible for the amount of time spent on homework, yet the schedule is flexible enough to accommodate almost any family routine. The place and time of day that is routinely set aside for homework will vary among households in order to accommodate family schedules, celebrations, and individual sports activities. With advance teacher approval, cultural activities may fulfill homework requirements.

How much effort is required by the teachers?

> "Once it is established, it runs itself."
> —JAN MCNAMARA, TEACHER, CHARLIE LAKE ELEMENTARY SCHOOL, B.C., CANADA

Teachers assign the work that they feel is valuable, no more make-work is assigned to fulfill arbitrary homework requirements or parental requests.

How much effort is required by the parents?

Parents are asked to be aware of the weekly time requirement and the time that their children spend doing homework. They need to sign their child's weekly homework schedule. Assignments requiring parent participation will vary among individual teachers.

How much effort is required by the students?

Most of the effort resides with the students. They are responsible for completing required homework and then for allocating time to work on self-selected projects.

How have parents, students and teachers responded to the Brady System?

Parents like this system because:

- Arguments about homework are reduced, expectations are clear, homework becomes a self-directed habit.
- Weekly communication about academic matters is maintained with the classroom teacher.
- Family priorities are valued.
- Meaningful work is accomplished.

Following implementation of the system at Sandburg Elementary School, parents offered these comments:

"I feel a lot more tuned in to what is going on in my son's classroom. I don't feel as powerless. With this system I can make a positive impact."

—DICK PIERCE

"What I liked was that the 'more' in 'more homework' wasn't just rote work or always just paper and pencil tasks." —JOY HAGEN

"My son digs in to finish his required work. We check it for completeness, then he can hardly wait to do what he wants to do. He is spending a lot more time 'learning'!" —ROB MCCAULEY

Teachers like this system because:

- Teacher priorities are valued. Assigned homework will vary among individual teachers based on their judgments as to what is important for their students.
- Responsibility is placed with the student where it belongs.
- The system is easy to monitor and evaluate.
- Communication with the home is maintained with a minimum of time and effort.
- Meaningful work is accomplished.

Elementary school teachers who have used the system say:

"I have found that this system saves class time. I don't spend so much time nagging kids. They remember to turn in homework on my homework return day. Most importantly, I start my class days positively, instead of checking up on who *didn't* do their homework. I became more organized. I planned my assignments ahead for the week, thinking of review or challenge, or both. The system helps me to be more in control.

"My students' parents felt as if they had an opportunity to talk to me by using the weekly homework form. They think the homework system is wonderful. I've received very enthusiastic responses." —MARILYN WOODS, TEACHER, MONTE VISTA ELEMENTARY SCHOOL

"It's a no-fail system with built-in success. My students felt like they had ownership of their time, they had a choice. This has been a big motivator. This system is a training process for life. Students take responsibility for stimulating their own minds.

"I like the way that I'm able to communicate weekly with parents, especially about reading, giving nudges when necessary. I can tell if parents and their children are taking an interest, and are communicating about school.

"Parents have come back to me when their children have moved on to middle school. One mother said she loved it because her son knows how to manage his busy schedule, he knows how to plan ahead and fit everything in on his own. She commented that he learned this with our homework system in elementary school." —ELLEN MAUPIN, TEACHER, MONTE VISTA ELEMENTARY SCHOOL

"Once the routine is set up, parents see the value of keeping in touch with what their child is learning and doing at school."
—M. REIMER, TEACHER, CHARLIE LAKE ELEMENTARY

Students like this system because:

- Their choices and interests are recognized and valued.
- Expectations are clear.
- Meaningful work is accomplished.

At Monte Vista Elementary School in Monterey, fifth grade students who used the Brady System for the first time evaluated their experience:

"It works a lot better for me. Last year the homework was supposed to take you forty-five minutes. It only took me five minutes. This system encourages kids to think more. The homework you give doesn't always take forty-five minutes but makes you think up more ways to do homework. It also teaches kids not to procrastinate until the last minute. I think it is an important system and should not be changed." —SHAUN KEMPSTON

"I like the system very much. Do all teachers do this system? I like it when you can add all the things, for example, playing an instrument or doing a project." — JOSEPH VELASQUEZ

"I like the way we do homework in this class because everyday we don't have to copy down things on the board and waste lots of time when we could be reading. I also like the way we get to choose some of the things we do. I like building things and doing science projects to fill my extra time."

—CAROLYN UWATE

"I enjoy reading a lot and do quite a lot of work a day and it is nice that work can get appreciated in this way." —ALICE VEKSLER

"It seems to work better than anything I have experienced and I hope you keep it up until you stop teaching. I think you should try to get other teachers to do the same." — ANDREW BAO

"I think this way of homework really stretches your ability to think. It really gives kids independence so they have to figure out what they are going to do with their time. Instead of just knowing what to do, you have to take responsibility. I really enjoy this form of homework."

— GREG BOGER

"I think it's great. I think it gives us responsibility. This homework system is totally perfect. I think you should give us more required work. It's hard finding things to do I think you Mrs. Brady should give us a list of books you recommend. All in all this is the best homework system I personally have had the pleasure of using." —JONATHAN YU

"I think it's a good idea how we're doing it now. That way we don't get to say, 'oooh, I lost my homework,' we just bring it in the homework envelope." — LISA ESPARZA

"I think that this homework system is pretty good because not every night I can do homework. (I play a lot of sports.) I think pluses and minuses are good ideas because they show how much we work and how little we work. Maybe forty-five minutes should be raised, forty-five minutes is fourth grade." —TYLER POTTER (a fifth grader at the time of this quote)

"The way that you do homework has been my favorite yet. I like the way that you let us decide what we want to do and when. I also like how you can include something that you enjoy like reading. I think we have just the right amount of homework so we have the responsibility to do what else we want. I don't think you should change it in any way." —COLIN TORREY

"I think the homework Monday through Friday is great because some of the people can do all of their homework in one night. The forty-five minutes a night is great but I think you should make the minutes higher." —AMY BARRERA

"The way this homework system works is really great. It's not like other classes where 'this is your work' and that's that, but it lets you think of your own things to do. Even though this system is great, it is not excellent. I think you should give a little more homework so we'll be prepared for 6th grade. It's just my opinion toward this so if you don't change this I'll understand." —DIANA HIDAJAT

I like the way we do homework. I like the selection of things we can do. I think you should keep doing this. Oh, and a few more things, I like the grading system, how there are pluses and minuses and we get points for pluses." —ZIBRAN BEY

Students like the routine requirements for home study and independent projects. Most students also appreciate recognition for effort or time on task in the form of a homework grade. Many want to tackle additional challenges.

Were there any negative responses?

Parent responses to the Brady System are overwhelmingly positive. No negative comments about the homework system were obtained on parent surveys. The overwhelmingly positive response is particularly encouraging since the system was brand-new at the schools in which the surveys were undertaken. Parents see the system as an improvement.

Teachers who use the system indicate that it takes a bit of work to get it running in a routine way, but after that, it's well worth the effort. The initial effort includes describing the system to parents and students at the beginning of the year and sending home reminder notes during the first few weeks. Class meetings or grade level meetings at the beginning of the year for parents and students are excellent opportunities to introduce the system.

> "My students' parents weren't recording the time spent on homework until I sent a letter home explaining how important it is to establish study skills, since then I've gotten nearly 100% cooperation!" — BARBARA IRWIN, TEACHER

> "The system is worry-free for the kids and me. The envelope, schedule, accountability for time, every-

thing together, helps kids to be organized."
—MARILYN WOODS, TEACHER

"This is a trouble-free system, easy for me to manage."
—ELLEN MAUPIN, TEACHER

"My students had to get used to the idea that they had to finish my homework first, then they could do the self-choice activities. It's going smoothly now."
—BARBARA WOOLSEY, TEACHER

What adjustments do students need to make?

Only three students out of Suzanne Brady's 1992 Monterey class of twenty-eight fifth graders wanted to make changes in the homework system. Their comments illustrated the difficulty that some individuals may encounter with the new approach to homework.

"I don't really care for the homework system because of the way of having to choose what you are going to do that day. I would rather take homework one night and bring it back the next day. And I would like to be graded on how well I did instead of getting graded on how long I did my homework over the week."—Fifth grade student

Students new to the system will need time to develop confidence in their ability to choose and carry out academic assignments. All students are still expected to complete teacher assignments, which will receive first priority. It is important to remember that these assignments will receive evaluations in some form according to classroom practice. For example, on a math assignment students will still be given feedback about the number of math problems completed correctly. Writing endeavors will still be evaluated for content, grammar, and structure. Students' grades and evaluations in specific subject areas will indicate the quality of their current work. They will not receive a grade on some of the self-projects that they choose to undertake. However, the system always credits time spent, thus giving students encouragement to be independent and creative. Independent efforts are valued by the school in a tangible way but the system does not create a bookkeeping nightmare for teachers. Time and effort become linked with visible and meaningful accomplishments.

Because some students are unused to being responsible for making choices, they may find it difficult. Some are also worried that their choices might not be good enough. These students benefit from lists of recommended activities from which to make choices and also from teacher guidance. When students and families understand the reasons for requiring self-choice and routine study times, their fears will be allayed.

Is the system flexible?

Teachers require short-range assignments as well as long-range projects. Some subjects benefit from daily versus weekly review. For example, math work usually requires immediate feedback. Long-range assignments are necessary to develop other abilities, such as research or writing skills. The homework log helps keep students organized and on top of both kinds of assignments.

Parents who worry that their children are not acquiring the skills they need become homework advocates when they understand how the system increases study time and productive output. For example, Suzanne Brady's students view editing and revising of written work as an expected and often-practiced form of homework. Students develop a positive attitude toward editing. It is simply part of the writing process, not a once-in-a-while thing to do. Editing is a valuable activity, and they receive time credit for doing it. Reading for enjoyment is also high priority homework. In Suzanne Brady's 1991-1992 fifth grade class, the number of books read per student ranged from twelve to one hundred twenty-six. "Short" books are counted only as "partial" books. The average for the year was twenty-five books per student. The average has been similar for the six years that the homework system has been in use.

One student said:

> "I think this form of doing homework is much better than taking homework home nightly, but I would like to know why you give us so much freedom?" —STEVE TARENTINO, FIFTH GRADE STUDENT

When students and parents understand how important motivation and independence are in promoting academic achievement, they support required self-choice activities. All partners need to know the reasons for participating in the system. The homework system encourages perseverance, independence, and flexibility. These are all characteristics of creative and productive individuals. The goal of the Brady System is to promote development in all three areas.

Another student commented on the system's flexibility: "I think that this system is pretty good because not every night I can do homework. It's hard to fit in sports and I really like sports."

The Brady System is based on minimum daily time requirements but students and their families may arrange the study times to fit their schedule and family priorities. For the student quoted above, the schedule was flexible enough to accommodate participation in sports. This student spent twice as much time on other nights and sometimes chose to use free time on weekends to catch up.

Flexibility in classroom structure is important in other ways as well. One important measure of flexibility is the option for students to move ahead when they need challenging work or a creative outlet. Another measure of flexibility is the option for some students to spend more time on difficult concepts without being penalized for a slower pace. The Brady System provides an additional means to incorporate these options into the classroom structure.

One student objected to any teacher-assigned work:

> "I think we should look out into our world and find our own homework to work on like read, write letters to relatives, stuff like that. I think this because when I get home from school to do homework, I don't understand something about it. I think about it a while and after some time it's all figured out. Math homework isn't fun, reading is, and reading is much more important." —ALEXA WALTER, FIFTH GRADE STUDENT

Students learn best when we build upon their areas of strength. School becomes a user-friendly place when students' interests are acknowledged. The route to this student's heart is through reading. It is important to acknowledge her interest. Reading is not an isolated skill. Efficient readers are also developing analytical thinking skills that are involved in mathematics. However, it is also necessary to provide frequent opportunities to practice math and to provide examples of connections between math and the real world. The homework system rewards student efforts to think things out. The requirement to spend time working on teacher-assigned work is beginning to pay off for this student.If she thinks about it for a while, she can figure out the math. Through the system of reward for time spent she is being rewarded for making the effort to think through math problems, rather than being penalized for taking more time to complete the assignment or for getting it wrong. She is thus more likely to revise her opinion about math.

Another student who was beginning to connect effort with improvement in a subject area described math homework in the following way:

> "I think the homework system is good but it is sometimes difficult for me to do, like math. The homework you gave us, the math, was hard for me to do but I got the hang of it. So maybe I will improve in those things." —STEVEN SINGH, FIFTH GRADE STUDENT

One student recommended improving the system by:

> ". . . putting more than three teacher assignments on the schedule and, if you can, give homework on Sunday or Saturday." —JOHN TALAMANTEZ, FIFTH GRADE STUDENT

In general this student comment, and others like it, are appeals for more homework and more guidance. Many students and parents worry about building competency. What the system does is help these students learn how to use their own time well. The student does not design his or her curriculum. The system requires a variation from the norm: "Choose some things for yourself, be accountable for your choices to the classroom teacher and to your parents." It is scary for some students to accept responsibility for their learning, but the result is greater self-confidence.

What are the key elements?

Key features:

- All students are required to spend a minimum amount of time.
- Minimum time requirements are specified.
- Students are accountable for time spent.
- Parents and students know what is expected.

Key ideas:

- Homework assignments are clearly relevant from the teacher's viewpoint.
- Self-chosen work is personally relevant to the student.

Effort and motivation are related. When students are not afraid to make mistakes, their effort increases. With sustained practice in valuable activities, competence increases. With increased competence, motivation is enhanced. This system makes the relationship clear.

What might my child's weekly homework schedule look like?

All students in a given elementary classroom will have the same teacher-assigned work. At primary grade levels, teachers will probably provide schedules with the class assignments written in at the top of the form. At upper elementary grades, teachers may require students to write in assignments. Every child's filled-in schedule will be different. Children will be writing in the number of pages that they read in their books, the amount of time spent on teacher assigned work, and on their own projects. Differences will be the norm, children will come to expect them, just as they will come to expect effort. This system is the road to excellence, not to the kind of competition that requires someone to lose before someone can win. Everyone wins.

Homework Log

Kindergarten

15 minutes per day

Required Homework: Share your "I like to . . ." book with your family. Bring your pet picture in by Thursday.

Monday: I read the book I made to Mom and Dad.
(I read it twice. We talked about it too.) 20 minutes

Tuesday: Dad read *The Fantastic Mr. Fox* to me. 20 min.
Drew a picture of my fish tank. 10 minutes

Wednesday: Colored my fish tank picture. 20 minutes
Dad read *The Fantastic Mr. Fox* to me. 20 minutes

Thursday: Dad read *The Fantastic Mr. Fox* to me. 20 min.

Student Signature ______________ Total time: 110 min.
(60 min. required)

Parent Comments:

Homework Log

1st Grade

20 minutes per day

Required Homework: 10 spelling diary words

Illustrate one of your Autumn Haiku poems.

John, Practice your subtraction facts with your Mom for 10 minutes each night this week, using the game I showed you today with the Q rods.

Monday	subtraction game 10 minutes spelling diary 10 minutse Mom and I read *Dinosaurs*, pages 1-15, 15 minutes
Tuesday	subtraction game 10 minutes *Dinosaurs*, pages 15-25, 20 minutes Drew a picture for my Haiku poem 10 min.
Wednesday	subtraction game 15 minutes Drew a picture for my Haiku poem. 30 min. Wrote letter to grandma and sent a copy of my poem and picture. 15 min.
Thursday	subtraction game 10 minutes worked on my rocket model and launched it with my Dad 120 minutes

Student Signature ______________ Total time: 265 min.

(80 min. required)

Parent Comments: The game worked very well. Are there any more we could do together in math?

Parent Signature______________________

Homework Log

2nd Grade

25 minutes per day

Required Homework: Bring your invention in for the inventor's workshop on Thursday.

Math Graph Project

Monday: Wrote birthday thank you notes to Grandma and my Uncle 25 minutes
Finished gluing my invention 10 minutes
Started my Math graph 20 minutes

Tuesday: Finished my invention display 30 minutes
Dad helped me fill out my inventor's notes 20 minutes

Wednesday: Painted my invention 30 minutes
Worked on the story problems for my math graph 20 min.

Thursday: Worked on my math graph questions 20 min.
Mom read *Matilda* by Roald Dahl to me (pgs 1-23) 35 min.

Student Signature ________________ Total time: 210 min.
(100 min. required)

Parent Comments:

Parent Signature______________________

Parent Signature______________________

Homework Log

3rd Grade

30 minutes per day

Required Homework: Math pgs. 15-18, Math Project

Memorize a poem for Microphone Day

Monday: Math, pgs. 15-16 30 minutes

Shel Silverstein Poem "I Wonder Why Dad is So Thoroughly Mad?" 15 Minutes

---

Tuesday: After school Science Class 60 minutes

Wednesday: Math, pgs. 17-18 25 minutes

Poem 15 minutes

Thursday: Poem 15 minutes

Read *Return of the King* by Tolkien pgs. 123 - 158 60 minutes

---

Student Signature ________________ Total time: 225 min.

(120 min. required)

Parent Comments:

Parent Signature______________________

Homework Log

4th Grade

40 minutes per day

Required Homework: Covered wagon due by Friday

Write a diary entry for your pioneer (three paragraphs)

Math page 31 (A and B)

Monday:	Math page 31A 20 minutes Worked on covered wagon 60 minutes
Tuesday:	Finished covered wagon 60 minutes Watched The Civil War on PBS 60 minutes
Wednesday:	Pioneer diary 30 minutes Math 31B 30 minutes
Thursday:	Pioneer Diary 30 minutes Chess club 60 minutes

Student Signature ____________________ Total time <u>330 Min.</u>

(160 min. required)

Parent Comments:

Parent Signature ____________________

Homework Log

5th Grade

50 minutes per day

Required Homework: Finish research notes for science report (Due by Friday!)
Math page 43, 1-5, 15-22

Monday:	Checked out books from the library on electric circuits and drew 4 diagrams of circuits 90 minutes
Tuesday:	Math 1-5 20 minutes Band concert (I played the sax) 60 min.
Wednesday:	Worked on science notes 30 minutes Read *Pool of Fire*, pages 22-30 20 min. Math 15-22 20 minutes
Thursday:	Finished science notes 30 minutes Practiced saxophone 20 minutes Read *The Pool of Fire* by J. Christopher, pages 30-50. 60 minutes

Student Signature ____________________ Total time: <u>350 min.</u>
(200 min. required)

Parent Comments:

Parent Signature ________________________

Homework Log

6th Grade

60 minutes per day

Required Homework:

Map work for Geography
Newspaper Article due Wed.
History Unit Test on Friday!

Monday: Cartooning workshop 60 minutes
Found and Read newspaper article 20 min.

Tuesday: Cartooning workshop 60 minutes
Worked on Geography Map 30 minutes
Took notes for history test 30 minutes

Wednesday: Chapter questions 80 minutes
Reviewed History notes 20 minutes

Thursday: Reviewed history notes and chapter questions 60 minutes

---

Student Signature ________________ Total time: 360 min.
(240 min. required)

Parent Comments:

Parent Signature________________________

What are some recommended self-choice activities?

Individual classroom teachers will provide guidelines for independent projects. It is to be expected that teachers, even within the same school and same grade level, will encourage different homework activities. Teachers and parents at Sandburg Elementary and Charlie Lake Elementary suggested a variety of activities for self-choice projects:

- Art: lessons, exhibits, museums, creating images
- Community Projects: environmental activities, tutoring
- Computer Projects: keyboard practice, computer-aided design, geography games
- Current Events: reports, discussion, editorial writing
- Educational Hobbies: chess clubs, rocket building, map making, story-telling, dramatics
- Foreign Languages: classes, language tapes
- Home Projects: measuring (kindergarten and primary cooking and carpentry activities), informational television programs with pre-approval of parent or teacher. To count as homework, television programs must be related to an educational hobby (for example, an art program), or an interest in a subject area, such as biology, (for example, National Geographic), or a unit of study (for example, PBS' "The World

at War," "Arctic Exploration")

- Math: math puzzles, practical problems, fact practice, math labs, tutorials, budget, or financial management
- Music: composing, concerts, performances
- Reading: fiction or nonfiction, alone or with an adult or sibling
- Science: experiments, exhibits and demonstrations, classes
- Writing: letters, diaries, reports, creative writing

The above list is not meant to be exhaustive nor are these learning activities to be used as substitutes for mandatory, teacher-assigned projects.

In Suzanne Brady's classroom, acceptable self-choice activities have to pass the Brady Test.

Student: "Will (a Boy Scout merit badge, a concert, thank you letter to my Grandmother) be acceptable as homework?"

Mrs. Brady: "What did you learn by (working on the badge, going to the concert, writing the thank you note)?"

Student: "Well, I learned . . ."

If the student convinces the teacher that learning took place, the activity will be accepted as self-choice homework.

At first glance, the self-choice activities seem like a random list with no connection to classroom organization. However, many of the students' self-chosen projects will be integrated under the umbrella of a general class theme or area of study.

Students also need the opportunity to pursue choices that are unrelated to prescribed curriculum. Personality traits found to be characteristic of creative people are perseverance, independence, nonconformity, and flexibility. The tools and skills used by most people for solving daily problems may not be so different from the tools and skills used by individuals engaged in highly creative endeavors, ". . . but their sustained commitment to their queries transforms the power of their tools and the magnitude of their achievement." (John-Steiner, 1987). If we are to foster creativity along with high achievement, we must allow individuals the opportunity to pursue their interests.

Is the homework system compatible with current classroom practices?

The Brady System is compatible with what teaching professionals describe as a constructivist emphasis. A constructivist classroom will have some or all of the following qualities:

- Subject matter is often integrated and/or theme-based, and interconnections between subject areas are explored in order to boost student understanding and skill.
- Problem-solving, questioning, and thinking skills are emphasized.
- Student interests are encouraged.

- Techniques involve building on student strengths.
- Primary resources in some subject areas are emphasized rather than a strict reliance on text books.

In classrooms with a constructivist emphasis, assessment plays an important role in improving the curriculum. Under the Brady System, students collect valuable data about their study habits. At a glance, teachers know how much time any one student is studying, what assignments are taking the most time, and what are student areas of interest. Data regarding overall classroom study patterns can pinpoint what areas are receiving the most attention and whether or not some critical areas are being overlooked.

The homework system provides help in dealing with one of the thorniest issues in education. How do we enable students to develop their interests and to move ahead as far and fast as their ability and interests allow, without swamping teachers with impossible demands? One way is to incorporate student-directed enrichment activities into the classroom structure. The will and ability to choose projects that have personal meaning are critical in the development of creativity. Teachers cannot prescribe projects in large and diverse classrooms that will fit every level of ability and every interest. However, the classroom can be organized to encourage student choice of independent projects.

As we strive to improve our system of education, the solutions that rise from the ranks of the frontline professionals are prime candidates for adoption. These solutions must then stand the test of critical review: Is this technique compatible with what we know of learning and behavior? The Brady System holds up well. It is simple to implement, but not simplistic. The underlying principles are well-supported by research. Educational research is most valuable when it is at the service of teaching professionals rather than the other way around. Too often, administrations try to impose solutions from the top that may or may not be useful in the eyes of the teaching staff who will be asked to implement them. An experienced teacher was the theoretician and diagnostician who developed the Brady framework. The system evolved from years of classroom experience.

Will the Brady System really have the desired outcome? The following chapters provide the reader with the means to judge its effectiveness.

CHAPTER 4

WHAT DOES RESEARCH HAVE TO SAY ABOUT HOMEWORK?

Before revamping our schools' homework systems, and asking our students to spend more time in home study, it is important to ask whether improved study habits will have the desired effect.

Does homework have an effect on achievement?

Homework has a powerful effect on the achievement of students from grade four through high school (Cooper, 1991, 1989; Keith, 1986, 1987; LaConte, 1981; Turvey, 1986). This is particularly strong for high school students (Foyle, 1984; Keith & Page, 1985).

Research below the fourth grade is sparse, but usually positive. There is evidence that, at early grades, homework improves arithmetic computation and problem solving. However, routine drill and assignments beyond the ability or resources of the primary student can have negative effects.

Studies suggest that homework improves achievement for students in the lower elementary grades as long as attention is paid to motivational factors (Paschal, Weinstein, & Walberg, 1984; Wolf, 1979). That is, students should understand the value of the assignment and they should have the ability to respond to the assignment in a way that guarantees some kind of success. Especially at the primary grade levels (kindergarten through third), comments and credit for time spent and assignments completed result in more effort and greater productivity than do grades.

This does not mean that homework needs to be individually prescribed. For example, all students in a primary classroom may be asked to write an essay on the same topic. Perhaps, after reading a book about a boy who has an imaginary dragon for a friend, students may be asked to write about a make-believe buddy. All students are potentially able to respond at some level to an assignment of this nature. Student feedback should include credit for effort, reinforcement for individual accomplishments regardless of skill level, and suggestions about what to do next.

Under the Brady System, a student who responded to the above assignment would receive credit for time spent. Next, the student would receive feedback about his work. For example, a teacher might say to a primary student, "You used lots of descriptive words to describe your imaginary friend. I felt as if I could see it too. I also noticed that you remembered how to use capitals and periods in your writing. That's great. Next, I'll show you how to write dialogue." The message that the student internalizes is: "I'm a writer. I know how to do some things well and I know what I need to learn next." In contrast, the message that is given to a primary level student when he or she receives a low grade on a writing assignment is, "I'm not very good at this." The outcome is usually lower production and less effort next time he or she is asked to write. The solution to this problem is not to lower standards so that students are earning A's . The solution is to give them credit for time spent, then to share real techniques with students at a level they can absorb, and allow them to progress as far and as fast as their ability and motivation allow.

A direct connection between homework and test scores at primary grade levels (kindergarten through third grade) has not yet been established (Keith, 1986). However, "In elementary grades students can be given homework assignments meant not so much to foster achievement as to promote motivation and good study habits, to dispel the notion that learning occurs only in school, and to allow parents the opportunity to influence their children by the value they place on education." (Cooper, 1989, p.181) Most researchers agree that motivation and success rate are important factors at primary grade levels.

Does homework affect achievement in all subjects?

Research on the general topic of time variables supports the assumption that children age ten and older benefit from regularly assigned homework in a variety of subjects, i.e., science, reading, math, history, and geography (Gettinger, 1984; Frederick and Walberg, 1979; Wolf, 1979). For elementary students in grades four through six, time spent doing homework was an even better predictor of achievement than measured intelligence, especially when willingness to spend time on a subject was high (Frederick & Walberg, 1980).

Positive effects on the achievement of junior high school students have been found for five to ten hours of homework a week. High school students show little effect with less than one to five hours of homework per week, but markedly improve with homework of five to ten hours a week and above (Cooper, 1989).

Private schools in the United States often assign more homework than do public schools. Relatively higher amounts of time spent doing homework accounts for a consistent part of the higher levels of achievement on test scores for private over public schools (Coleman, 1982).

Does homework affect achievement for students of all ability levels and socioeconomic backgrounds?

Several studies have illustrated that homework is effective for students from all ethnic backgrounds (Keith & Page, 1985), for gifted students (Stanley, 1980), and for low-achieving youth (Frederick & Walberg, 1980; Keith, 1982). Students who are high achievers in school, even though their backgrounds are highly dissimilar, have several characteristics in common. They spend time in study, their families encourage study time and they see learning as intrinsically rewarding. Students who are at risk for school failure have been helped by programs that focus on study time as the key variable in improving the chances of success. One such program is discussed in the following chapter.

Should homework be assigned on a daily basis?

The conclusion that is warranted after reviewing the available studies is that daily homework results in larger positive effects than intermittent homework (Walberg, 1984; Walberg et al., 1985).

What kind of homework is most effective?

Unfortunately, most of the available research has focused on issues of quantity rather than on type of homework. The emphasis has been on how much homework students should be assigned versus what kind of homework is most effective. We do know that different types of homework are more effective depending on the type of skill required and the stage in the learning process. For example, at the initial learning stages, students may require more practice homework. When students become more familiar with a concept, less practice is necessary and assignments that require comparison, contrast, and application to new situations will be more appropriate.

A few studies have dealt with different kinds of math homework. Math homework that was designed to prepare students for new material or for practice of previously presented material led to higher test scores than homework that dealt solely with the content of the present day's lesson (Cooper, 1989). In other words, effective math homework will often include some review of material that has already been presented to students. This does not mean that students need to do rows of the same sort of problem, but a brief reminder of previously mastered concepts is helpful.

Another effective math homework technique is to encourage students to apply previously learned concepts in new situations. For example, before learning how to add fractions, students may do preparation homework by adding fractional numbers on a number line.

In general, the average junior high or high school student doing preparation and practice homework will score higher on tests of achievement than students doing homework based only on the current day's lesson. Students who have had exposure to practice assignments continue to score at higher levels on tests measuring mastery of concepts even after significant time has elapsed between tests.

Practice and review results in high confidence levels and the maintenance of skills at high levels. A few practice problems at regular and frequent intervals are sufficient to keep skills honed.

How should practice homework be used?

The most traditional and familiar type of homework is the practice exercise (LaConte, 1981). As noted in the previous section, both practice and preparation homework result in higher levels of achievement than no homework (Foyle, 1984; Foyle & Bailey, 1984). However, it is important to keep in mind the distinction between initial and higher levels of mastery. At the basic skill level many children require practice to master the subject being taught. At higher levels, despite the strong tradition of this type of homework, practice is highly questionable in terms of effectiveness and utility.

Far too often practice-type homework assignments are dull, unimaginative, repetitive exercises that produce little besides student boredom. Few students feel challenged when asked to perform a page of essentially similar mathematical operations or to underline subjects and verbs in twenty or thirty sentences. The able student frequently masters the skill quickly and plods mechanically through the remainder of the exercise merely to complete it, while the less able student, more in need of practice, soon gives up. Overemphasis on rote drill and memorization is not helpful for skill development or motivation.

In general, there is evidence of negative effects of too much routine practice, yet such assignments are linked to superior academic achievement at initial stages of learning. When students are just beginning to understand a concept, more practice will be necessary. Later, only brief reviews at wider and wider intervals will be necessary.

Should teachers individualize homework assignments?

In general, teachers do not need to prescribe individual homework assignments for students. There is no clear indication that individualized homework assignments are more effective than group assignments. H. M. Cooper, acknowledged expert in the area of homework, reviewed the available homework studies on individualization and concluded that, "Given the enormous added burden individualization creates for teachers, its benefits were minimal" (Cooper, 1989). Individualization of homework assignments burden the teacher unnecessarily without achieving the desired results.

This finding does not mean that individual explorations are unimportant. A substantial body of reported experiences attests to the interest, excitement and growth that individual explorations can promote (La Conte, 1981). It simply means that teachers do not need to take on the responsibility for prescribing individualized homework for each student in every area of study.

Some students require extra help to achieve desired goals in certain subject areas. Other students require opportunities to explore materials at an accelerated pace. One often hears parents of motivated students say, "My child is not challenged by the curriculum. He/she needs in-depth work and is held back by the slow pace of the class." There are several ways a teacher can respond. One way is to provide teacher-directed enrichment in the form of accelerated courses for students who illustrate aptitude and motivation. Another method is to encourage student-directed enrichment. Both types of enrichment are important.

A homework system that promotes effort, measured by completion of teacher-assigned work and self-choice work, can help students become more independent of the class pace. If, from kindergarten through grade six, students were held responsible on a regular, routine basis for teacher-assigned work and for explorations that expand on their unique interests and talents, we would hear more parents say, "My son/ daughter was not challenged by the (math, science, writing, literature etc.) curriculum, so she/he chose to undertake projects that did present a challenge."

This can happen when the classroom is structured to encourage individual initiative. Capable students often report that self-chosen projects were the most rewarding in their public school experience. This in no way implies that teacher-directed enrichment through accelerated courses is unnecessary or unimportant. High-level options and challenging courses should be made available at all grade levels. The homework system is just one way of preparing more students to take advantage of these high-level options when they reach middle school and high school.

In order to enable more students to succeed in challenging course work at upper grade levels, classroom practices at the elementary level should:

- Allow students to move between ability groups.
- Improve the study skills of all students.
- Increase exposure to scholarly processes like editing, revising, using information sources, and applying problem solving techniques to new problems.
- Encourage students to attempt new and challenging tasks without fear of making mistakes.

The Brady homework system does all of the above by emphasizing effort and scholarly process.

Should homework be graded?

Homework in general appears to improve achievement, but grading homework at higher grade levels and feedback on homework at lower grade levels has an even stronger impact (Cooper, 1989; Paschal, et al., 1984).

When homework is assigned without feedback, it appears to raise test scores. Students who score near the 50th percentile on normed tests advanced to the 60th percentile. But when feedback is given, homework appears to raise student achievement from the 50th to the 79th percentile. "This graded-homework effect is among the largest discovered in educational research literature." (Walberg, 1984, p. 76) In these early studies, grades meant a letter grade that indicated how well a student was doing in a subject area. As studies became more precise, it was apparent that the graded-homework effect could more appropriately be called the homework feedback effect: when students receive feedback that indicates what was done well, and what needs improvement, learning is enhanced. The simple presence of a letter grade without comments does little to help students expand their learning. Teachers do not need to grade every assignment, but some type of credit or acknowledgment needs to be given for all completed assignments.

At lower grade levels, specific comments and suggestions for improvement may be far more effective than grades. Students will benefit from concrete suggestions that acknowledge the students' successes and use the mistakes to identify the direction of future effort.

Parental checking for homework completion also appears to add to its effectiveness (Levine & Worley, 1985). When parents check homework, and use a non-judgemental and non-critical approach, students tend to develop a more thorough approach to homework. Positive consequences include simple reinforcers such as parent praise and encouragement. Praise statements that focus on student effort, regardless of the outcome, are particularly helpful for elementary-age students. For example, "I'm really proud of your hard work on that project."

Rewards for homework completion are an area of controversy. Several prominent researchers including Ames (1990) and Cooper (1989) believe that extrinsic rewards may have possible negative effects. Extrinsic rewards for learning seem to get in the way of forming the belief that learning is important and rewarding for its own sake. For example, an early pioneer study called "The Making of a Scientist" found great economic differences in background among the scientists studied. However, the one common characteristic among the scientists was the emphasis placed on learning for its own sake by their parents. Later studies corroborated the finding. Emphasis on a belief in learning for its own sake, that learning is rewarding and satisfying, is a common value held by practicing scientists and artists (John-Steiner, 1985). This is also true of the parents of high achieving students (Chaplin, Choy & Whitmore, 1992).

If rewards are needed initially to establish study habits, reward for effort is probably preferable than reward for good grades. For example:

"You did such a good job starting your homework without arguing, that we have 15 extra minutes to read tonight What do you want me to read to you?"

"You did all your homework this week and spent extra time on your science project. Let's go to a movie tonight to celebrate."

"You really worked hard on those tough math problems all week. I'm really proud of you."

When students are consistently held accountable for minimum study time, most will learn to do their homework appropriately. External incentives can be phased out. Verbal praise for effort is always appropriate.

What kind of feedback on homework assignments is most effective?

It has been established that feedback is very important, but the type of feedback which is most successful is as yet unclear. There are many feedback strategies: comments versus grades, continuous versus intermittent feedback, verbal praise versus rewards. The effectiveness of each strategy remains to be demonstrated (Cooper, 1989). In general the effectiveness of different forms of feedback will vary with teacher preferences, student age, and the goal of the assignment.

Comments can be very powerful, especially when they indicate which aspects of the assignment have been mastered, or which skills have shown improvement, and what specifics need to be tackled next in the learning sequence.

Positive comments about behavior are more effective than negative comments. ("I like the way you started your homework in plenty of time today" versus "Why can't you ever do your homework without me having to remind you?") Intermittent praise sustains positive behavior more effectively than constant praise. Parents do not have to praise children every time they complete homework assignments or every time they spend the required number of minutes in study. Teachers also do not have to praise or evaluate every completed assignment.

Under the Brady System, homework completion is something that parents and students will eventually take for granted. However, adult interest in students' school activities and honest praise is always appropriate and is encouraged. For example, "I'd love to learn how you solved that problem. Can you show me how you did that?" or "I'm impressed by how much you've learned about Greek heroes. Who is your favorite?"

CHAPTER 5

HOMEWORK AND ITS ENVIRONMENT

Television viewing interferes with achievement for children from many different backgrounds and socioeconomic levels. Several studies have found a negative relationship between children's creativity and imagination and heavy doses of standard commercial television programming.

What effect does television have on achievement?

The studies dealing with the relationship between television viewing and achievement have uncovered a negative relationship that persists across research designs, even when background characteristics of subjects are controlled (Williams et al., 1982)

Merrow (1985) found that American children between six and eleven years of age watched, on the average, twenty-seven hours of television a week (the equivalent of two months a year). Walberg & Shanahan (1983) found that high school students were averaging between four and five hours of homework a week and watching at least twenty-eight hours of television per week. Some researchers have speculated that homework may improve achievement in part by displacing time spent watching television (Paschal et al., 1984).

A representative sample of 58,000 high school seniors reported three or fewer hours of homework per week (High School and Beyond Longitudinal Survey, 1983). This level of commitment is depressingly low when compared with figures for television viewing. In 1982, fifty-seven percent of the same seniors had reported spending two or more hours per night during weekdays watching television, and thirty-seven percent reported watching three or more hours per week night. The situation has not improved a decade later. In 1993, forty-nine percent of eighth grade students interviewed and thirty-four percent of the twelfth graders interviewed averaged three to five hours of television per night. Thus, many high school students may spend more time per night watching television than they spend per week on homework. Hamburg (1992) reported that young people in the United States between the ages of seventeen and eighteen years of age on the average have spent 15,000 hours watching commercial television in contrast to the 11,000 hours they have spent in school.

How does parental involvement effect student achievement?

Parental involvement has important effects on student achievement (Bloom, 1984, Walberg, 1984). Academic achievement is increased through parental involvement in the form of:

"verbal encouragement and interactions regarding schoolwork" —MAJORIBANKS, 1983

"expectations for school performance" —SEGINER, 1983

"reinforcement of academic performance, and general academic guidance or support." —BLOOM, 1984

These parents expect their children to complete assignments as well as time permits. The parents are also interested in school activities, and they set aside routine times for study.

In a longitudinal study of the effects of parental involvement, Epstein (1983) found significant increases in elementary students' achievement, when parents listened to students read, read aloud, and participated in at-home learning activities. These students had the greatest gains in reading skills. She also found that students who liked to talk about homework and school with their parents and who were not made tense by working with a parent had higher math and reading skills. They were often considered by their teachers to be homework stars. Children who didn't like to talk about school or who became tense when working with a parent had lower academic scores and were more likely to be discipline problems and homework problems.

In Epstein's study of elementary grade levels, low-achieving students spent more time completing homework, and parents spent more time helping them, then did higher achievers. She interpreted this finding to mean that the schools were using parents to reach children who were not succeeding. The increased amount of time that low-achieving elementary-age children spent on homework may have increased their frustration with school. Clearly, assigning more of the same kind of homework to an elementary student who is having trouble, without knowing something about that student's attitudes and about parent-child interaction in that family, will not solve the student's problem. Students who are not succeeding even after they expend effort need additional help.

Is the Brady System compatible with parenting research?

Recent research in child development has identified characteristics of effective parenting. Parenting styles have been divided into three general categories; authoritative, authoritarian, and permissive. Authoritative parenting styles have clear advantages over authoritarian and permissive styles. In general, authoritative parents stress firm consequences but there are clear rationales given for rules and standards. Standards are based on parental values but children's wishes are considered and active listening takes place among all parties. Families in homes where effective parenting systems are in place are not free from strife, but routine ways to settle differences are practiced. Mutual respect governs exchanges. Authoritative parenting styles result in children who are more independent, who score higher on measures of thinking skills, and who exhibit greater leadership and social skills.

Other parenting styles such as authoritarian and permissive, do not fare as well as authoritative styles. Authoritarian parenting is characterized by rigid parental control. Decisions are made with little or no family discussion, rules are handed down by dictate. Authoritarian parenting styles in general result in lower scores on measures of independence, leadership, social skills and thinking skills than authoritative styles. Permissive parenting styles that demand little or no responsibility result in the lowest scores on measures of social and thinking skills (Baumrind, 1987).

The Brady homework system dovetails very nicely with authoritative parenting styles. For example, students are required to work within established guidelines and they are held accountable for their effort but they are also given choice in some of the work that they undertake. The goal is not to control students, but to enable them to be in control of themselves.

There are numerous parenting techniques offered by professionals in education and psychology for parents who want to help their children succeed in school and who also want to stop the cycle of nagging and arguing about homework. These recommendations have many recurring themes. Five of them are presented here.

THEME # 1

Building your child's self-esteem is the most important factor in helping your child develop his or her potential. A good environment for learning is one in which the child is not afraid to make mistakes. The parent sets the stage with praise and encouragement and with routine, habitual requirements for study. The content of school assignments is less important than students developing attitudes about themselves and about school. Building a love for learning and an interest in pursuing studies independently is more important than completion of 100 percent of assigned worksheets. To help maintain high self-esteem during study time:

- Keep the tone at study time positive.
- Listen attentively and show enthusiasm.
- Provide encouragement, focus on the improvements.
- Defuse competition between siblings by emphasizing effort and enjoyment of learning rather than grades.
- For all children, but especially for the child who has academic difficulties, emphasize the importance of individual strengths and interests.
- Emphasize successes, acquisition of a skill rather than grades, completion of a difficult assignments or portion of a difficult assignment, and meeting self-set goals. If your child does not meet a goal, respond with compassion. "I can see that you're unhappy about this assignment."

Avoid anger or punishment. Focus on what the child learned by his or her mistakes, concentrate on the next steps to take.

- Take the pressure off by asking questions that show you are interested, not to test your child.
- Read with your child for enjoyment. When your children want to read on their own, continue to show interest in their books, ask them their opinions, encourage them to talk about their books. Set aside reading time for the whole family. Turn off the television during study time and model reading for enjoyment.

THEME # 2

Requiring effort does not hinder the development of self-esteem. In fact, the two may often go hand in hand. As students practice, they become more competent. When they learn how to develop their interests, they become less vulnerable to comparisons with other children. If students are required to spend study time, they learn to set personal goals and to take concrete steps to accomplish them.

Responsibility is something that needs to be taught and practiced. When children are held responsible for their choices, they learn how to become more in control of their own lives. In order to foster greater independence:

- Don't do your children's work for them. When parents become too involved, the message is that children are not capable and their effort is not important.

- Let them experience the consequences at school if they choose not to complete assignments.
- It is helpful to the student who lives with joint custody parents to reach family agreement about homework routines. Routines should be as similar as possible in both households.
- If a child declines help during regularly scheduled study time but panics at bedtime because work is not done, refrain from badgering or scolding but be firm. Natural consequences are a great teaching device. Students will learn to budget their time and become better able to estimate how long different assignments take if they have to face the consequences of their own lack of effort.
- Be available to help at homework time. Children will usually ask for, or accept your help, as long as it is not forced on them.
- Most primary students do not require incentives to do homework if a routine has been established. If a child needs encouragement to get started, choose a reward that he/she will appreciate, or let the child choose between acceptable alternatives.
- Refuse to be pulled into arguments about home-

work. Simply state your expectation. "It's homework time. I want you to start your homework now." If your child argues, restate your expectation. "I understand, but I want you to do your homework." If restating the expectation doesn't work after three tries, back up your words with action. Cantor and Hausner (1987, p. 76) give the following example that is appropriate for students from grades four through twelve: "You have a choice. You can do your homework during your scheduled homework time or you can choose not to have privileges." Privileges may include watching television, listening to music, partaking in social activities, using the phone, driving the car, etc. Privileges are reinstated when routine homework time is reestablished by the student.

- Try not to make vague or meaningless threats like, "I mean it! Next time you argue with me about homework you're on restriction for a month" or "Do your homework or else! I'm not kidding!" Being consistent will give the clear message that study is important. Children may choose to test adult resolve with tactics such as crying, tantrums, or hostility. Stand your ground, let your child know that these tactics will not work and in the end your child will still have to do the homework. When children understand that the caregiver is not going to back down, they will respond. If a homework partnership has been established between the children's home and school, the testing period is usually brief in duration.

- Children may balk if homework is too difficult or boring. If it is too difficult, a solution should be worked out with the teacher. It is easy to sympathize with children who truly dislike some assignments. You may even agree that an assignment is boring and pointless. Sometimes teachers will accept alternate assignment suggestions. But it is not always the specifics of the work that we are concerned with, it is the process. If your child is unlucky enough to be stuck with uninspiring work it shouldn't be used as an excuse not to do homework. Under the Brady System, some self-choice work is usually just around the corner.

THEME # 3

Most books on homework contain tips for setting up a study area. Students need a comfortable space at home in which to complete assignments. This place should consistently be used as the study area. In time, just being in the usual spot will trigger effective study behavior. It may be the kitchen or dining room table or a desk in the student's room or some other appropriate area that has a writing surface and materials like pencils, paper and a dictionary. Let your child choose a place to work. Provide the proper tools, good lighting, ventilation, and a flat surface. Do not allow television, and limit phone calls during homework periods. In our computer age,it is helpful to have access to computers and software such as spell checkers. Many schools are now making computer lab availableafter school for students.

An inner-city foster family with six teenaged students under their supervision used the following techniques to promote academic success. The living and dining room area was turned into a study area every week night. Each student had his or her own study space. The teenagers were responsible for helping each other. Their foster care parents left out drinks and a snack each night and helped when they could. In this particular case, these young people lived in a neighborhood that was dominated by gangs and violence. All of them finished high school with high marks. Four are doing well in higher education and two have developed effective entrepreneurial skills.

Additional recommendations for study areas are:

- The student should be able to do his homework without leaving the security of his homework place.
- Develop a Drop Spot, an area that belongs to the student (preferably near the usual exit door). It can be a hook on a wall or door, or a place on a counter or table where children always place

their backpack. When homework is finished, homework is placed in the back pack. On the way out the door the student grabs the pack to take to school. The homework cycle is complete, helped along by routine.

THEME # 4

Homework, like all activities students undertake, has a better chance of getting done if it is scheduled into the daily routine. Help young students fill in their timetable and record completed work. Consult with older students about their schedule. During study time other activities should cease. However, some children actually do better with some background noise. If your child asks to listen to music while he studies, experiment. See if the arrangement works for your child. If it doesn't, the radio can always be turned off.

- Wait until your child asks for help before becoming involved in homework assignments. There are two reasons for becoming involved; the first is when your child is stuck and has tried hard, the second occurs when homework is complete and your child wants an adult to check it over.

- Stop at a reasonable hour. If your child is having trouble finishing homework before bedtime, help him or her set a schedule, and check the calendar ahead of time to judge how much time will be needed.

- Try to include some regular time reading together. Reading is special private time with a child that benefits other areas of your relationship.
- Designate a time to study. Plan ahead for occasions when study times need to change because of other activities.
- Be available but don't intrude. Sit and read or complete your own work during study time. It helps when the adults go without television for some of the time.

THEME # 5

Many children lose patience when they are overwhelmed by a problem. If your child is frustrated or overwhelmed, help him or her break assignments into manageable chunks. The steps for tackling tough problems are summarized below:

- Have them restate the homework assignment in their own words. Let your child explain his or her understanding to you.
- Help your child list the steps in the order required to tackle the problem. (If the assignment is writing, use the list as an outline.)
- Pinpoint the trouble spots.
- Avoid becoming annoyed over repeated mistakes. Do something else if things become tense.

- Review the basic concepts (number facts, scientific method, fingering on a musical instrument). If you are also stumped on the concepts, tell your child. He will appreciate the fact that he is not the only one who doesn't have it down pat. Turn to the section in the text that explains the basics. Look at examples of similar problems. Review the steps in the example problem and apply them to your problem.
- Make sure your child has the necessary background material. Is another book needed? Material from the library?
- Ask yourselves if the answer or conclusion is reasonable. Help your child check his or her work. Was something left out? Recopied incorrectly?
- Still stumped? Take a break, get a snack, or exercise and come back to try again. Call a friend who is working on the same assignment. Ask how she solved the problem.

If after going through the problem-solving steps, your child is having great difficulty completing an assignment, attach a note to the homework and make an appointment immediately with your child's teacher. Regular monitoring of homework can prevent your child from falling behind. Ask for help from your teacher or counselor if your child has trouble completing two assignments in a row.

Another important facet of a successful homework process is sharing positive techniques with parents for working with their children at home. There are several excellent books like *Homework Without Tears* by Canter and Hausner (1987) which provide sound homework tips for parents. Several elementary schools have shared parent solutions with other parents in opening day forums. Parents from Charlie Lake Elementary School in British Columbia suggested the following sensible ideas for reducing homework stress:

"I find that if I give my child the choice as to when she can do homework, it helps. But I limit the choices to these three: right after school or before or after supper."

"Homework at our house is done at the kitchen table just before supper. That way I'm always there to work with my child."

"Take turns with both parents. That way, kids feel that both are interested and if one parent is frustrated, the other can take over. Anxious parents can effect a child's work in a negative way."

"Never belittle. If you say they're doing poorly, they lose interest and feel bad. If they associate feeling bad with reading, they won't want to read."

"Being a working mom with three children, I often ask the older children to help the youngest with his homework."

"Because we drive quite a way, my girls often read during the trip. Also, if we have math facts to practice, the car is a great place to do that. This also goes for spelling."

All of the above recommended homework tips are more easily put into practice under a homework partnership program like the Brady System..

How can we help children who do not complete homework?

Teachers are often concerned about children who do not complete assigned homework, or whose work is completed in a manner far below their ability level. Self-help training has been shown to improve completion levels, especially for children who have little or no support from home (Fish & Mendola, 1986). An important component of self-help training is charting study time. A habitual, routine assignment schedule also fosters success for children who are struggling to complete work.

A group of Oregon researchers (Quackenbush et al., 1989) have addressed school failure.

> "Many children needlessly fail in public school. They have adequate intelligence and academic aptitude but they do not complete and turn in work. Their self-esteem plummets and they do not seem capable of recovery without adult help."
>
> —QUACKENBUSH ET AL., 1989

They recommend that:

1. Students chart on-task time in each subject with a stopwatch.
2. Students be required to study five nights a week.

3. Students be told there is no such thing as not having homework and are directed towards methods of working on homework and study.

The use of time as a measure of homework compliance is very helpful to students who have experienced little or no support from their home environment with regard to schoolwork. Students become better at focusing on the value of the task to be learned.

The goal is to increase practice time and experience with academic tasks. Greater exposure to academic tasks in the areas of reading, writing, and logic, is vital to the success of all children. The gap between high and low achievers in the amount of time spent in practice outside of school becomes a tremendous disadvantage as early as the fourth grade. Many children have ability, but lack skill due to insufficient opportunity to practice.

Academic stress increases for students who have trouble finishing homework. A combination of leisure reading assignments and self-choice projects can be effective in reducing stress for children (Pickens, et al., 1986).

Do parent training programs actually reduce the homework hassle?

Children with academic and behavior problems who do not regularly complete homework benefit from programs involving parent training.

Results of programs designed to help parents work with their children have been encouraging. Turvey (1986) reported that after one such program, children's academic scores improved and teachers reported fewer behavior problems. Walberg, Paschal, & Weinstein (1985) reviewed twenty-nine controlled studies of home interventions which included training in homework help. Ninety-one percent of the comparisons favored subjects in the homework training groups over control groups. Although the average effect was two times what might be expected due to differences in social class, some programs had effects ten times as large (Walberg, et al., 1985).

Moderate parental supervision of students at higher grade levels appears to lead to higher class standing; more involvement appears to be beneficial at lower grades. An important daily homework activity often recommended by many teachers and reading specialists is reading aloud to primary grade children. However, research examining the effects of formally casting parents in a teaching role is inconclusive. Considering the claimed positive and negative effects of parent involvement in instruction, it is probably best for teachers not to promote direct instruction by parents unless the parent is provided with training in appropriate techniques. Involvement in homework as a shared parent/child task can be a difficult arrangement. Even parents who are skilled teachers may discover that it can be difficult to teach their own children because of their emotional attachment (Cooper, 1989).

However, it makes good sense for parents to support their children's interests. Indeed, parent support of homework dramatically increases the probability of academic achievement. Many biographical accounts depict the influence of a parent or older mentor who profoundly influenced the development of talent. Exchange of ideas and willingness of a parent or another adult to work together on a shared project gives young students a sense of direction and hope. John-Steiner (1987) calls these discussions among individuals with shared interests an important part of the informal "apprenticeship of the mind." Students who willingly work with a parent or adult in "unscheduled" enrichment sessions often find that their achievement soars in the area studied.

What characteristics of the home environment foster academic achievement?

The "curriculum of the home" is an important influence on learning (Walberg, 1985).

Parents who provide a place to study, and who convey the feeling that completion of homework and learning in general is important, have children who express more satisfaction with school and who achieve at a higher level.

The main characteristics of this kind of environment are:

- A consistent emphasis on homework and study.
- Encouragement for students to assume responsibility for their own learning and that of others.
- Parental belief that learning is inherently rewarding and worth the effort (Mackenzie, 1983).

Other, more recent studies of high-achieving children have also pinpointed similar cultural elements that promote achievement (Caplan, Choy, & Whitmore, 1992). Students in these studies came from Asian immigrant families who speak English as a second language and from low-income African-American families. The critical cultural elements involved in their academic success were:

- Homework clearly dominated household activities during weeknights.
- Parental involvement included reading regularly to young children.
- Love of learning was rated by students and their parents as the major factor accounting for academic success.
- Families stressed the importance of effort rather than ability. Parents in the households of these high-achieving children emphasized believing in the ability to effect change and attain goals.

Children who have acquired a high level of academic skills upon completion of high school simply do homework, and their families encourage and support their efforts in tangible ways. Starting at elementary school, these students realize that the common refrain "I don't have any homework" isn't going to work. They read books, or practice math, or write stories to resounding echoes of their parents' praise for their efforts. Students from these diverse families thrive in schools that operate under a wide range of philosophies and with teachers who use a variety of teaching methods. They come from high and low-income backgrounds and from all ethnic groups.

CHAPTER 6

CULTURAL DIFFERENCES IN ATTITUDES TOWARD HOMEWORK

Several countries rank above the United States on achievement in science and math. The top one percent of students in the United States rank thirteenth out of thirteen countries in biology, eleventh in chemistry; ninth in physics; eleventh in algebra; and twelfth in geometry and calculus (Office of Educational Research and Improvement, United States Department of Education, 1993). The homework practices of students in the higher-achieving countries reveal important differences. American children spend fewer hours in school and devote less time to academic activities than do children in many other countries (Chen & Stevenson, 1989, Garden, 1987; Stevenson, Lee, & Stigler, 1986).

Chen & Stevenson (1989) and Stevenson, Chen & Lee (1992) investigated the attitudes about homework in three countries, the United States, Japan, and China. Their subjects were first, third, and fifth graders drawn from private and public schools and represented similar socioeconomic levels.

How much time do children in the United States, China, and Japan spend doing homework?

Chinese teachers reported many more homework assignments than Japanese teachers, who in turn reported more homework assignments than American teachers. First graders in Taipei were assigned more than twice as much homework as first graders in Japan and more than ten times as much homework as first graders in Minneapolis. Chinese teachers assigned more than twice as much homework for fifth graders as Japanese teachers, and four times as much as American teachers. Estimates of assigned work obtained from mothers in all countries were consistently above the estimates of their children's teachers.

The finding that Japanese children spend less time on homework than Chinese children was unexpected in view of the popular image of Japanese children being closely supervised at home by an educationally-oriented mother. One explanation is that Japanese elementary school children, to a greater degree than American or Chinese children, spend their after-school time attending classes (*juku*) where they may be given additional schoolwork. Forty-six percent of Japanese fifth graders attended some kind of after-school classes or received private tutoring. The percentages were lower for Chinese (fourteen percent) and American (ten percent) fifth graders.

How much homework assistance do children in America, China and Japan receive from parents?

The amount of time that family members helped their

child with homework each week was consistently higher for Chinese than for American families. In Chinese families seventy-five percent of the first graders and ninety-two percent of the fifth graders were given help by their mothers. In the American sample sixty-six percent of the first graders and seventy-eight percent of the fifth graders reported that they received help. The most surprising aspect of these data were the results for Sendai, Japan. Japanese mothers did not report large amounts of time spent directly helping their children. In Japan the percentages were forty-nine percent for first graders, sixty-nine percent for fifth graders. The involvement of the well-known *kyoiku mama* (education mom) apparently does not include a great deal of direct assistance with homework. Japanese children's estimate of how much assistance they received at home was in agreement with their mothers!

The lowest percentage of time reported by fathers in helping their children with math homework was in the United States sample. Only twenty-four percent of the fathers in the Chicago sample estimated that they helped their child on mathematics homework fifteen minutes or more a day. In Japan the percentage was thirty-two percent. Taiwan reported thirty-six percent, and China reported forty-four percent.

What is the correlation between the amount of homework and the student's attitude towards it?

Of the groups studied, Chinese children in Taipei reported the most enjoyment of homework and American children had the most negative feelings. In all three cities, fifth graders liked doing homework less than first graders. The percentage of Chinese students who liked homework was sixty-six percent, versus sixteen percent who did not. The percentages for American students were nearly opposite; sixteen percent of American fifth graders liked homework, versus sixty-one percent that did not. Most Japanese children (sixty percent) were neutral on the subject, but twenty-nine percent did not like homework.

American children at first, third, and fifth grades indicate that they do not enjoy doing homework and their mothers believe they must intercede in order to see that the children complete it. These attitudes are in sharp contrast to those of their Taiwanese and Chinese counterparts, who perceive homework to be important, useful, and enjoyable.

Do teachers' attitudes about homework differ among the three countries?

On surveys that deal only with the subject of homework, American teachers indicate that homework is important. However, when ranked on a scale which compares homework with other teacher activities, it is relegated to a low position.

In the Stevenson and Chen studies, teachers were asked how important they considered homework to be for pupils' academic achievement in relation to fifteen other items such as drill, examinations, teacher's availability, physical punishment, discipline, memorization, and individual instruction. American teachers assigned homework an average rating of 4.4 on a nine-point scale (1 = very unimportant, 9 = very important). This was in contrast with the average of 7.3 for Chinese teachers and 5.8 for Japanese teachers. In fact, the rating by American teachers for homework put it a second from last among the sixteen items; only physical punishment received a lower rating.

Academic success is strongly emphasized in Chinese and Japanese societies. Both parents and teachers in these two countries perceive the additional practice and review provided by homework as a useful contribution to children's success at school. American teachers, in contrast, relegate homework to a low position in the hierarchy of activities involved in students' academic success.

In the three countries studied, who is considered to be primarily responsible for completing homework?

Responsibility can be allocated to the child or assumed by the parents. American mothers appear to be less likely than Chinese and Japanese mothers to believe children should assume primary responsibility for completing their homework. Only eight percent of American mothers thought it was solely the child's responsibility. In contrast, thirty-two percent of the Chinese mothers and forty-three percent of the Japanese mothers assigned the sole responsibility to their children.

What are the differences in beliefs about innate ability versus effort?

Stevenson, Chen and Lee (1992) present evidence of cultural differences in the emphasis given to ability versus effort in accounting for the academic achievement of elementary children. Chinese and Japanese fifth graders and their mothers, following long-held tenets of Asian philosophy, stress the importance of hard work as the route to success. American mothers, to a much greater degree than Chinese and Japanese mothers, emphasize the importance of innate ability.

The same belief was true of eleventh graders and their parents. At grade eleven Chinese and Japanese students retained their belief that hard work was of primary importance. Their American peers retained their strong belief in the importance of innate ability, as a greater factor in academic success than effort.

What are the differences in cultural beliefs about students' performance in math?

Students and teachers in all three countries were given a list of factors that might influence student performance in mathematics: a good teacher, innate intelligence, home environment, studying hard. When asked which was the most important factor, these were the results:

- More Chinese parents (fifty-nine percent) and Japanese parents (seventy-two percent) than American parents (twenty-seven percent) thought studying hard was the most important factor.
- Ninety-three percent of Japanese teachers selected studying hard as the most important fac-

tor. Only twenty-six percent of the American teachers selected this response.

- American teachers (forty-one percent) chose innate intelligence as the most important factor. Fewer Chinese teachers and only seven percent of the Japanese teachers made this their first choice.

- When asked to indicate how strongly they felt about the statement "Everyone in my class has about the same natural ability in math," American students disagreed to a significantly greater degree than did Chinese or Japanese students. American mothers strongly disagreed with the statement and Japanese and Chinese mothers were more neutral.

Is time spent on homework related to academic achievement among the three countries?

The amount of time spent on homework by students in the different countries was positively related to academic success. Both Chinese and Japanese children did more homework and also achieved at significantly higher levels in math and science. This does not prove that math success is directly related to homework. It does makes sense that greater exposure to study and practice yield tangible results. It is also safe to conclude that strong beliefs in the importance of effort would lead to greater emphasis on completing homework which, in turn, leads to gains in achievement.

Children in cultures which view homework as a valuable activity, and who spend consistently greater amount of time studying obtain higher scores on achievement. If the assignments are interesting, and children can see they are useful, this form of practice can greatly facilitate academic achievement. Such a situation exists in Taiwan and China, where children do a lot of homework, say they enjoy it, and exhibit high levels of achievement.

However it should be noted that differences in time spent on homework do not clearly relate to academic success within the different countries studied. For example, within each country, for primary and elementary students in first through fifth grades, children who spent the most time on homework were not necessarily the most effective students. Some of these students were struggling to keep up. For these students, some form of tutoring (peer tutoring, adult tutoring before or after school, ability grouping for greater teacher intervention) was necessary in order to help these students over obstacles. Conversely, children who spent too little time on homework did not benefit greatly from the time they did spend.

Although assistance from parents may generally have a positive effect on children's achievement, children with lower levels of achievement at the elementary level in each culture received the greatest amounts of parental assistance. Thus, the amount of assistance within each culture varied according to the child's needs. The amount of assistance offered by parents in China and Japan appeared to depend on the importance placed upon academic achievement and on the amount of help deemed necessary for children to learn basic skills.

The achievement gap between the performance of Japanese and Chinese children compared to children in the United States is greater in 1990 than it was in 1980, even though a 1986 study of first and fifth graders in the United States, Japan and Taiwan found no innate intellectual differences among the children (United States Department of Education, 1993). In 1990 only 4.1% of the Chinese children and 10.3% of the Japanese children had scores as low as the American average on standardized tests.

Using average scores might not be the most appropriate way to compare level of achievement in different countries. Another measure of academic performance compares the top ten percent of students in each country. In math, top students in Minneapolis performed similarly to the averages for Japanese and Chinese performance. This is especially worrisome because Minnesota students rank high among the states in mathematics achievement, and Minnesota has the highest percentage of students graduating from high school in the United States. When problems are found in Minnesota, more severe ones might be expected to occur in many other states (Stevenson, Chen, and Lee, 1992).

The high level of satisfaction expressed by American mothers when asked about their children's academic achievement illustrates large differences in expectations. Few Chinese and Japanese mothers expressed high degrees of satisfaction with their children's academic performance, compared to the forty percent of American mothers who did express high satisfaction. In 1990 even more United States mothers indicated high levels of satisfaction with their children's performance than in 1980. American mothers were aware that American education was in trouble, but did not associate the phenomenon with their own children. American students echoed the same attitude. Despite publicity on the need for education reform, for upgrading standards, and for assigning more homework, mothers of fifth graders were no more enthusiastic about instituting changes in 1990 than they had been in 1980.

All of the industrialized countries, with varying degrees of success, strive to help children from low income families gain greater access to educational opportunities. The education systems in Germany, France, and Japan leave fewer students behind than systems in England and the United states. Green and Stedman (1993) point out that Germany, France, and Japan have high expectations for all students. Their curricula embody these expectations. Rarely in these three countries does one find some schools where students are expected to work hard and other schools where little is expected of students.

These countries have standards-driven systems but they do not educate all their students to the same high level. Many of the differences in achievement are the result of poverty and inequality of opportunity. Nevertheless, these systems consistently do better with more of their students, including low-income students, than the current system in the United States.

It is not enough to demand high standards without giving children the tools to achieve them. A homework system like the Brady System is a concrete way to put the tools for achievement in our students' hands.

Does a high level of academic performance come at a great psychological cost?

Critics of the success of Chinese and Japanese students often suggest that their high levels of performance come at great psychological cost. Some of this criticism appears to be based on informal reports and old data. No recent comparative studies support this belief. Stevenson, Lee and Chen (1992) sought such information by asking students in three countries to indicate the frequency of stress, aggression, depression, and somatic complaints such as being unable to sleep. Researchers asked about the frequency with which students felt nervous when taking tests or when the teacher handed tests back.

American students, not Japanese students, reported the most frequent feelings of stress, academic anxiety and aggression. The most common source of stress was school. Stress related to school was mentioned by seventy percent of the American students, more than three times as often as four other major sources: peers, family, sports, or jobs. Japanese students reported the lowest frequency of occurrence of all these characteristics. The data obtained do not support the Western stereotype of Asian students as tense young persons driven by relentless pressures for academic excellence. Had the Asian students in the study exhibited frequent indications of psychological disturbance, it would be reasonable to argue that high standards for academic achievement may occur at unacceptable costs. Rather, it was the American students who were more likely to express indications of distress. The researchers suggested that American students do not have a clear idea about the importance they should place on education. Chinese and Japanese students are expected to devote themselves primarily to their studies. American students, in contrast, are faced with many opposing demands. For example, more than three times as many American as Asian students have after-school jobs (seventy-four percent versus twenty-one percent). More than twice as many have dates (eighty-five percent versus thirty-seven percent).

Stevenson, Chen and Lee (1992) reported the achievement scores of a large sample of American kindergarten children which exceeded those of children from China and Japan. The authors attribute this finding to the greater stimulation provided by American parents. Yet, from first grade on, American children begin to lag behind on the usual measures of achievement. Throughout their schooling American students have demonstrated equal ability and even exceeded the scores of Asian students when tested with items not based on school curriculum. Students from all cultures have the ability to do well in their studies. However, the expectations that different cultures place on study and learning differ enormously.

The differences in homework practices found in the above studies cannot be attributed to uneven sampling. Enrollment in school is universal among first and fifth graders in all three countries and the percentage of adolescents enrolled in high school is similar, if vocational schools are included, as was done in the study. The achievement gap is real.

The likelihood of improving our children's chances for a satisfying future depend at least in part, on changing self-defeating attitudes. There are no scientific indications that one ethnic or cultural group is inherently more capable than another. Ability is evenly distributed across ethnic group and socioeconomic levels. However there are great differences in expectation for study and homework across cultures, and real differences in beliefs concerning the effects of ability versus effort.

The results from the cultural studies do not indicate that we should duplicate the Asian system of education. Some educators in Japan and China worry that their methods are producing skillful mathematicians who are not sufficiently creative (Matthews, 1993). What we need to do, is examine prevailing attitudes and ask ourselves how we can build upon our strengths. The Brady System is one positive step that encourages innovation as well as diligence.

Do children's attitudes about intelligence affect their achievement?

Some bright children start avoiding academic challenges when they reach junior high and stop liking some or all of their classes. Parents report an increase in conflicts about time spent in study. Teachers report that the progress of their classes is slowed by the large numbers of students who do not complete homework. One of the reasons for the decline can be explained by children's beliefs about the nature of intelligence in general and their beliefs about their own intelligence.

According to Henderson and Dweck (1990), most children start out in their early school years with an **incremental view of intelligence. That is, they think a person gets smarter by trying hard and learning step by step.** But by fourth grade young children may begin to believe in an entity theory. According to the **entity view, you are born with a certain amount of native ability that determines how smart you are.** A link between these beliefs and student grades develops when students move on to junior high.

Henderson and Dweck found that students who believed that effort was important performed at a level equal to, or better than their elementary school performance. Perhaps most surprising, even the incrementalists who exhibited low confidence earned higher grades than the children who had confidence that they were intelligent due to native ability. In fact, students who believed in innate ability and had high confidence at the start of seventh grade showed the most pronounced decline in grades of any group.

Incrementalists report that they feel smart when they put effort into something, when they don't understand something and then get it, or when they figure out something new. Entity theorists however, point to times when a task is easy for them, when not much effort is required, when they do not make mistakes, or when they finish first. Entity theorists then are caught in a serious bind when they face challenging tasks. They tend to think of themselves as having failed as soon as they reach a difficult problem. They attribute difficulty to mean lack of ability. So they avoid situations in which they might not look smart, rejecting the chance of learning something new if it involves risk of error or confusion. Entity theorists, those students who believe that intelligence is a fixed trait, tend to pursue the goal of proving that they have it. They are more vulnerable to loss of confidence and to falling into a helpless pattern when faced with difficult tasks.

In contrast, children who believe that you have to try hard to learn tend to plan strategies to overcome failure as soon as they run into difficult problems. They begin to improve their problem-solving strategies through increased practice as tasks become more difficult. The incrementalists see effort as something that activates ability and they are more likely to set goals and persist in the face of difficulty. Challenging academic tasks are seen as opportunities to "get smarter," rather than as threats to their self-image.

By fifth and sixth grade some students, even though they may be doing well in school, are developing beliefs that will later make them vulnerable. These beliefs are changeable. Dweck and Henderson demonstrated that students who had developed an entity viewpoint could develop a more incremental type viewpoint with training in problem-solving. Low-confidence students can learn to see errors as sources of information for future efforts rather than evidence of low ability, especially if they are not penalized for making mistakes. Homework systems that reinforce effort rather than a perfect product can help shape positive motivation patterns, similar to the incrementalist view.

CHAPTER 7

PURPOSES OF HOMEWORK

In order to create effective homework systems, it is important to understand teacher, student and parent expectations regarding the purposes of homework.

How similar are American parent, student, and teacher beliefs concerning the purposes of homework?

STUDENT SURVEYS

American students indicate that the preparation and practice opportunities offered by homework are important in preparing them to reach career goals. Lack of time spent on homework is a major concern for adolescents, according to a major survey. The report titled *Voices from the Classroom* (1992) is based on a survey of 1,365 eleventh and twelfth grade high school students chosen to represent different geographic regions and school populations. The survey found that most students think that teachers are doing a good job but many think parents should be more involved in their offsprings' academic lives. Almost all of the student respondents deemed it important for parents to set study rules from grade school through high school, to support after-school instruction and to provide resources like trips to the library. Ninety percent of the students said it is important for parents to help with homework and eighty percent said it is important for parents to set study rules. Only twenty percent of the students described volunteer work at school (bake sales, chaperoning, etc.) as an important activity. Less than six of every ten children thought parents in their neighborhoods were "heavily involved" or even "somewhat involved" in preparing their children for school and schoolwork. More than seven of every 10 students thought their teachers were doing an "excellent" or "good" job. In general, students are asking their parents for more rules and structure regarding homework.

PARENT SURVEYS

Surveys of parent opinion have found that parents value homework because of the opportunity it creates for the "development of study habits" as well as for direct learning.

It is a myth that low-income and minority parents are indifferent toward their children's education. In a six-year study, Chavkin (1989) interviewed African American and Latino parents in six states. Ninety-five percent of those interviewed expressed a strong commitment to their children's education. These parents wanted to take a more active role in school decisions regarding homework, student evaluation and behavioral rules. Both teachers and parents were hampered by a lack of communication about homework.

Homework becomes an area of dissension within families when parents find themselves nagging their children to start their homework, or rushing them to finish it at a decent hour. Parents of adolescents find themselves in conflict with their students over time spent on activities not involved with school (Rolf and Muss, 1990). Conflict could be greatly alleviated by a planned homework system based on parent, student, and teacher teamwork.

Many parents of students at the junior high school level feel that their children have not developed good study habits. It is reasonable to conclude that elementary-age students could benefit from a homework program that systematically reinforces independent study skills and encourages effort, thus preparing them for more rigor at middle and high school levels.

TEACHER SURVEYS

When teachers identify general purposes for assigning homework (Palardy, 1988), their opinions closely match parents' views. That is, homework teaches students independence, self-discipline and responsibility. Many teachers believe homework is warranted for these reasons alone. Featherstone (1985) interviewed 3,000 teachers in city, rural and suburban Illinois schools. He found that eighty-eight percent of the teachers and students interviewed agreed that homework develops student initiative and responsibility.

The second major purpose stated by teachers is that homework increases student academic achievement. The most recent and most thorough review of research in this area (Cooper, 1989) provides support for this belief.

The third major purpose for homework is that homework fulfills the expectations of students, parents and the public. One writer has called this "the most powerful" purpose (Pendergrass, 1985). Gallup Poll questions (1985) revealed that the public favors more homework, that most students think homework is necessary, and that more than 95 percent of all teachers favor homework (Palardy, 1985).

Studies that deal with homework practice, as opposed to opinion, find that teachers in the United States place homework on a lower priority level that do teachers in other countries. This difference in practice may be due to the difficulty American teachers face when they do require homework. Many children simply do not complete homework assignments. Families need to know how to structure their home environment to support homework completion.

The fourth major purpose for homework is that it expands and eases time constraints on the curriculum. It allows students to have learning experiences in "real" situations such as the home, the city hall, or wildlife preserves, etc. as opposed to contrived classroom situations. It helps ease time constraints on the curriculum. In Japan "learning time" (school time plus homework time) averages fifty-two hours a week, fifty-three percent higher than the average learning time in the United States of thirty-four hours a week (Walberg et al, 1985).

Homework assignments will vary in style and content because learning in any subject area requires simple practice and complex thinking skills. When the purpose of homework is to foster achievement in a specific and well-defined area, assignments will focus on skills that require practice. When the purpose is to generate interest in a topic, and develop problem-solving skills, assignments should be more challenging, requiring the use of higher-order thinking skills and the integration of different domains of knowledge and experience.

Purposes of homework such as extending the school day will likely be more important in the higher grades, while those of increasing motivation and home involvement are more important for the earlier grades (LaConte, 1981).

Finally, homework can give parents insights into a school's philosophy, curriculum, and objectives. It can become a communication link about academic issues. Quality homework develops parent support for the school. In these days of shrinking resources, taxpayer support for education is essential.

What do professional reviews have to say?

Reviews of professional publications on the subject of homework reveal a consensus on the purposes of homework. The basic aim of homework should be learning how to learn.

Homework should help the student establish study habits and learning skills that can be used to become familiar with any new information (Turvey, 1986). To increase motivation, homework should stress student initiative and require imagination and creativity. For this purpose, long-term projects are more beneficial than practice drills.

Some researchers group homework into the following categories:

- *Practice Homework,* to reinforce skills or achieve mastery of a skill.
- *Preparation Homework,* to provide background for new material.
- *Extension Homework,* to expand upon in-class learning and to apply learning to new situations.
- *Creative Homework,* to integrate material from different disciplines in order to create new insights, solutions, and products (Cooper, 1989).

Assumed benefits of homework are widely accepted as truths in numerous educational publications. Based on classroom experience, many educators and parents ascribe to the following beliefs:

- Homework develops patterns of effort and concentration (Keith & Paige, 1985).
- Homework strengthens the bond between the home and the school (Friesen, 1978).
- Homework helps students learn to budget time, see a task through to completion, and to tune out distractions (La Conte, 1981).

What are the most commonly expressed objections to homework?

One of the few negative comments about homework

that has been widely quoted in the media comes from England's and Flatly's *Homework Do's and Don'ts* (1985):

> "Then too, kids need time to be kids . . . just getting kids to do homework becomes recurring ground for battle in many homes. In the background we hear chants of "Teach them discipline!" and "They must learn life is demanding!" We would submit that taking a cold shower teaches discipline too; and compared to doing homework until 11:00 p.m. three or four nights a week, it would probably do more to keep kids awake in school. As for learning that life is demanding, perhaps being in school is demanding enough. And if it is not, having the school day encroach on what might otherwise be family time may not be the solution." (pp.11-12)

When this paragraph has been quoted, what has generally been misunderstood is the fact that the authors, England and Flatly, are not against homework. Their major concern was simply how homework was implemented and how much. In the demand for more homework, children could become inundated with unreasonable amounts. Recent research suggests that this has not been the case. Consider especially the positive effects that ten hours and more of homework have on the attitudes and achievement of high school students (Cooper, 1989). The only inundation that has occurred has probably been in the area of television viewing. If families and children decide that homework is important, that it produces desirable outcomes, then many problems can generally be resolved. Several studies document the large time blocks that American children spend viewing television. These studies indicate that more homework time could become available with some adjustment to television viewing.

> "The homework suggestions that our Science Specialist sends home are great! My daughter loves doing the experiments for her 'self-choice' homework time. We've set down a new rule at home—our house is now a television-free zone from Monday through Thursday." —CHRIS IMORI BOLTJES

Most parental objections to homework also center around the issue of time commitment. The most commonly heard objections are:

- "Children work hard enough at school already without being burdened with extra work at home."
- "Students have many other important out-of-school activities that do not leave time for homework."
- "Homework interferes with family time."
- "Teachers 'bunch up' assignments, so that students will have too much to do on some nights and not enough to do on others."

All of the above concerns should receive careful consideration. Especially at the elementary level, unstructured play time is necessary for healthy development. Recreation is important at any age and it is important to budget time for it. The minimum time requirements recommended by educators (see the following section on Time Guidelines) are not so burdensome that they interfere with unstructured play at the elementary level nor with leisure and sports activities at older grade levels. Even with an overall upgrading of homework expectations for our students, the number of hours spent in school or occupied with schoolwork would be well below that of students in other nations who score well on tests of academic achievement and social adjustment.

Recent data studies do not support the belief that increased student responsibility for homework and higher expectations are accompanied by high stress levels. Leisure reading has actually been shown to reduce academic stress (Pickens, 1988). Time spent reading increases academic proficiency, vocabulary, and understanding of human behavior. It makes sense that reading homework may actually promote family unity rather than disturb it.

> "My son wasn't all that interested in reading until we started reading aloud for self-choice homework time. Now we're into the second book of *The Lord of the Rings* and we both forget to stop when the time is up. My wife has to remind us to quit because it's bedtime." —CHRIS LARSON

When schools promote homework partnerships, teachers and parents report heightened family rapport, reduction in stress related to school, and higher student self-esteem. The following comment by a teacher in a British Columbia rural school district is typical of reaction to the Brady Homework System:

> "I didn't want to implement the new homework system at first. Many of our students, like my own children, have long bus rides home and then have ranch chores waiting for them when they do get home. I believed that they had enough to do without doing more homework. But I tried the system and found that homework has become family time. We all sit around the kitchen table for at least a half hour or more and do our work together. It's great!" —TEACHER, CHARLIE LAKE ELEMENTARY SCHOOL, B.C., CANADA

Like sports activities, learning activities can be incorporated in the family routine rather than be seen as something separate that only happens in school. Pleasurable family activities, such as trips to the science center, model rocket clubs, plays, and art classes can be incorporated into a family homework routine as self-choice items.

If all students within a local school district are required to complete mandatory and self-choice assignments for at least a minimum number of minutes per week, the likelihood of conflict and parental nagging to bring about completion of assignments is greatly alleviated. The parent or guardian who oversees homework time can use the refrain, "Everybody is doing it," to their advantage. Parents also have a ready response for the ubiquitous student remark, "I don't have any homework" or, "I finished my homework at school." The response is: "Great! Now what are you going to choose to do for the remainder of your homework time?"

The message given to children by a homework policy that encourages personal choice and accepts unique family values is, "The life of your mind is something that you have a responsibility to develop. The school values your unique interests." Acceptance of individual interests in the form of self-choice assignments promotes bonding among family members, between families and teachers, and to the school in general.

School-wide time requirements can boost students' academic achievement and also reduce parental anxiety about the amount of time their children should be spending on homework. Time guidelines based on sound research and understanding of children's development can help alleviate the problem of the overly-scheduled child, as well as the under-challenged child.

At older grade levels the problem of "bunching up" homework so that students have too little to do on some nights and too much to do on others can be easily remedied with cooperation among teachers, parents and students. The remedy requires advance planning among teaching staff members regarding:

- Minimum required homework time per week per subject.
- School-wide coordination of expectations for the quantity and the quality of student written work.
- Communication with parents and students regarding homework policies and expectations.
- Course syllabi listing advance requirements and due dates for integrated assignments (assignments that cross subject matter).
- Homework calendars for student self-charting.
- Provisions for student accountability.

Some high schools routinely provide in-class time for students to complete homework assignments. In view of the low number of classroom hours and low teacher contact hours that prevail nationwide in our school system relative to other countries, this may be a mistake. We need to see our high school students spending fewer hours in front of the television and in low-skill jobs, and spending more hours in after-school study groups, peer tutoring, and engaged in school projects and practice.

Chapter 8
Homework Policies

In spite of the fact that homework is a variable that can be easily and economically adjusted for the benefit of students, very little effort is made to coordinate homework policies at the school and district level.

What information is available concerning homework policies that are currently in place in the United States?

In a recent survey of teachers and principals in one Midwestern state (Murphy & Decker, 1990), researchers found that teachers received very little support in terms of school-wide structures. Responses were received from 3,000 teachers in a random sample of Illinois high schools. Schools included rural, city, and suburban sites. Nearly two-thirds (sixty-two percent) of the teachers reported that there were no formal structures to assist them as they implemented classroom homework procedures. In fact, only fifty-seven percent of the schools even communicated their expectations about homework to parents. Parents were not involved in providing input for school-wide policies.

Given the frequency with which parental involvement

and support of the school's academic program is being uncovered in studies of effective secondary schools (Chubb, 1988), it would appear that schools are remiss in not tapping into this valuable resource.

Two recommendations resulting from the Murphy & Decker survey are the following:

RECOMMENDATION #1: STRONGER EFFORTS SHOULD BE MADE TO COORDINATE HOMEWORK THROUGHOUT THE SCHOOL.

Coordination among teaching staff members is one of the hallmarks of an effective school. Forcing teachers to establish policy on a room-by-room basis, and further, to be asked to promote accountability without parent support, is not in line with the principles that guide effective schools.

A homework policy that is balanced in terms of frequency and duration of assignments, purposes of student work, and types of skills and experiences, can only come about through the development and implementation of well-defined school policies. Each teacher should be enabled to see how his or her procedures fit into the homework structure of the larger organization.

RECOMMENDATION #2: INDIVIDUAL TEACHERS SHOULD NOT BEAR THE ENTIRE BURDEN OF ENSURING THAT STUDENTS COMPLETE HOMEWORK.

Accountability for completion of homework is an area where parent support is vital. A breach in the parent-teacher partnership over this issue is harmful to student motivation. A good deal of attention must be given to developing systems that support teachers and increase student accountability. These systems should include ways to increase parent awareness of their children's homework assignments. The schools in the Illinois survey were not taking advantage of parental interest and concern in relation to homework assignments.

The report also stressed the pivotal role the principal can take in implementing policy and coordinating efforts to help parents become more active participants. Clear expectations and information about ways parents can help their children with homework should be shared with parents.

The good news is that homework assignments in Illinois and California are increasing (Murphy & Decker, 1990; Guthrie & Kirst, 1988) and that teachers are extremely diligent in their review of homework: seventy-six percent of the teachers surveyed checked between eighty-one percent and one hundred percent of students' work, ninety-seven percent of the teachers who graded homework computed these marks into semester grades.

The bad news is that student responses to homework is low. Almost half of the students surveyed completed less than eighty percent of the assigned work. Given that most of the assignments were practice-type activities, a success rate of eighty to one hundred percent could be expected. Yet only thirty-nine percent of the students achieved this level of accuracy, and only six percent met the ninety percent or better level of success

Half of the teachers in the Murphy and Decker study

chose "textbook and questions" as the most commonly employed homework type. An additional twenty-five percent chose "worksheets." Two interpretations can be drawn from this information. It is possible that teachers are trying to provide concentrated doses of independent practice. It is also possible that the pattern reflects a lack of attention to higher order thinking skills.

What homework policy guidelines are recommended by researchers?

Cooper's recommendations (Cooper, 1989) are based on extensive reviews of homework research over the last two decades. His recommendations are as follows:

- Districts should state clearly the broad rationale why homework is given, why it is sometimes mandatory, and the general ranges for the frequency and duration of assignments.
- School policies should contain guidelines that describe the ways the homework policy will be implemented and monitored.
- Homework should be assigned at all grade levels. A mixture of both mandatory and self-choice may be most beneficial to students.
- Elementary students should be given homework even though it should not, below the fourth grade, be expected to improve academic grades or achievement test scores. Instead homework for young children should be expected to help

develop study habits, foster positive attitudes toward school and learning, and communicate to students the idea that learning also takes place outside the classroom. As such, homework assignments in the primary grades should be relatively short, should employ materials commonly found in the home environment, and should lead to successful experiences. In the primary grades (kindergarten through third) homework needs to be carefully given in content, scope, and quantity so that it does not become counterproductive. Motivation is important at these levels.

- Concentrate on building intrinsic motivation for homework. One of the most effective ways of doing this is to acknowledge student interests through self-choice projects.

- Homework should never be given as punishment. Using homework in this way implies that it is boring and aversive. If we have students do homework out of fear of negative consequences, we turn the situation into one that implies the teacher and/or parent thinks threats are required to get it done or else no one would want to do it.

- Keep comments about homework positive.

"I'm proud of the way you're taking responsibility for your homework."
"Your practice is really getting results!"

"You learned a lot doing that project. I'm impressed!"

- At the elementary school level a formal structure for communicating between the school and the home about homework assignments is necessary for routine compliance with assigned work.
- Parents can provide support for the school's academic goals by requiring routine study hours and by providing resources when needed (trips to the library for resource materials, provision of supplies, encouragement, etc.) For students who are involved in sports and extracurricular activities, advance planning and foregoing some hours of after-school jobs may be necessary for the long-term benefits of completing homework.
- Cooper recommends that parents sign work before it is returned to school. Author's note: Accountability can be enhanced if students self-record the "time spent" each day and parents indicate by signing their children's homework log that times indicated are accurate.
- A developmental progression for the role of the parent should be coordinated throughout all grade levels involving reduction of the formal role of parents in homework as students develop independent work habits. For younger children Cooper recommends that parents set aside a rou-

tine time period for homework. For older children it my be wiser to specify a time by which homework must be completed.

- Some flexibility to accommodate different learning styles and family schedules is beneficial. For example, Cooper contends that complete silence during time set aside for homework is not necessary for every child. Or some families will want to pre-plan homework times around sports practice and lesson schedules.
- Parents should be available to help with an occasional question, or to review assignments. Cooper's basic rule is: it is the child's homework, not the parents'.
- Individualization of assignments within classes is not a high priority. At this time there are few or no demonstrated advantages to individualizing mandatory homework. Developing individualized homework can create a time burden for teachers with little measurable payoff.
- Type of homework should be closely tied to the purpose of the assignment.
- All homework should be collected and reviewed in light of the reason for which it was assigned. For older students, the function of homework should facilitate the acquisition of knowledge and skills in specific topics.

- Especially at the elementary level, homework assignments should be successfully completed by nearly all students. Teachers do not need to grade all homework, but feedback is important. Although grading homework has been shown to be effective in improving achievement for older students, simply commenting on homework for primary level students may be more beneficial than grades.
- Assign homework on a regular basis. Daily work, Monday through Thursday, is more beneficial than intermittent homework.
- In general, grading should be kept to a minimum at the primary level. Comments and accountability are, however, important at all grade levels.
- For older students intermittent grading of assignments has been shown to be as effective as continuous grading. Studies that compared feedback strategies (grading, instructional or evaluative comment) reveal no clearly superior approach.
- Provide a consistent, habitual means of communicating homework requirements to parents.

What are Cooper's Guidelines for Teachers?

- Homework should have a clear purpose. What is to be learned from doing this assignment?

How will my students benefit from this assignment?

- Assignments should flow from the curriculum and should be an integral part of thecurriculum.
- Assignments should be clear: How are they to complete the assignment? What is the expected product?
- Determine difficulty level; individualize only as deemed necessary and/or beneficial.
- Variety is important. Unneeded practice and overreliance on one type of assignment should be avoided.
- Develop assignments at the primary grade levels with a high potential success rate in mind.

What homework time guidelines are recommended by experts?

In response to concerns about time guidelines, two prominent researchers, Keith (1986) and Cooper (1989) have suggested time guidelines for school homework policies.

Cooper (1989) recommends the following time ranges for mandatory assignments:

- Grades 1-3: one to three times a week, fifteen minutes.
- Grades 4-6: two to four times a week, fifteen to forty-five minutes.

- Grades 7-9: three to five times a week, forty-five to seventy-five minutes.
- Grades 10-12: four to five times a week, seventy-five to 120 minutes.
- All grade levels: additional voluntary assignments.

Keith (1986) recommends these time ranges for homework:

- Grades 1-3: ten to forty-five minutes per night.
- Grades 4-6: forty-five to ninety minutes per night.
- Grades 7-9: sixty to 120 minutes per night.
- Grades 10-12: ninety to 150 minutes per night.

Keith's time recommendations are greater at all grade levels. However, Cooper recommends voluntary assignments as well as required assignments. Self-choice assignments have some advantages that voluntary homework does not have. Self-choice assignments are assignments that students are required to do, as opposed to a voluntary assignment which a student may choose not to do. Students have the responsibility for deciding what the content of a self-choice assignment will be. Both self-choice and voluntary assignments have tremendous potential for developing budding interests and independence. However, self-choice assignments have the additional advantage of sending a clearer message about the importance of schoolwork and the notion of student responsibility.

If the time taken to complete voluntary assignments (or required self-choice assignments) was added to the nightly totals, Cooper's and Keith's time guidelines would be similar. School-wide minimum time requirements within the ranges recommended by either of the above researchers are reasonable.

CHAPTER 9

THE EIGHT ESSENTIAL QUALITIES

Effective homework policies share several important qualities. If the goal is to implement a homework policy that encourages self-esteem, academic achievement, and creativity, these qualities should be included.

Long-range Developmental Progression

Minimum time requirements should increase with maturity, reflecting the changing needs and abilities of students as they progress through the school system. Homework requirements become more complex with each level.

A coordinated homework plan for students from kindergarten through high school graduation can be developed through staff planning and parent input. Assignments should reflect the academic goals of the school community. In order to promote parent support, academic goals should be clearly communicated to parents and examined on a periodic basis. Academic goals may vary across levels. For example, at the primary level, teachers and parents may choose to adopt "love of learning" as the overriding goal that guides their behavior. Homework assignments at this level (kindergarten through third grade) will be designed to promote self-esteem and routine habits of study outside of the classroom. For instance, all elementary students will be required to spend time writing, and the writing assignments will be designed with student success in mind.

Upper elementary grades concentrate on increasingly complex academic skills and greater self-reflection. Students will be required to do more extensive revision of their work, and to produce lengthier projects. Some elementary schools require that students from first through sixth grade complete a "research report" once a month but these schools usually provide great leeway in the choice of subjects. Use of more complex writing techniques will increase with grade level.

By developing a planned, long-range homework system that encourages effort and practice, our students will be able to develop the skills they need in order to face challenges with confidence.

Teacher Autonomy

One of the characteristics of effective schools involves teacher autonomy (Wilson & Corcoran, 1987). The classroom teacher is the professional closest to our students and their parents. It makes sense that teachers require flexibility in order to tailor programs to meet the needs of students.

"Autonomy" implies that teachers are powerful program builders, that they have the freedom and responsibility to decide how they will teach core subjects. As trained professionals, they need the freedom to diagnose their students' strengths and learning styles and to prescribe the most effective way to achieve academic goals. When this autonomy is diminished, teacher performance diminishes. Teachers who are authoritative decision-makers in their classrooms and in the decision-making process of the school exhibit the following: higher morale, increased commitment to the school, improved management decisions, greater acceptance of change, enhanced cooperation among colleagues, and more effective enforcement of discipline (Corcoran, Hansen & Shidlowski, 1988).

The homework program advocated in this manual does not in any way interfere with the classroom teacher's methods, content, or decision-making. The system is not an agent for teacher behavior change.

> "Helping students with poor home study skills is conceived as a high-level parenting/behavior change problem, not a teaching problem. The key is to reach into the home, activate parental interest, and empower parents to become positively engaged in their child's education."
>
> —QUACKENBUSH ET AL., 1989

It is an agent for changing the way our families and students approach academic tasks. The system simplifies the homework management job for teachers and provides an objective method for increasing student accountability. The focus is on the student. The additional effort and responsibility for making choices resides with each student; the teacher-parent partnership shows the way.

This system does not require that teachers prescribe

individual assignments nor does it burden the teacher with undue record-keeping. It is the teacher's responsibility to see that homework assignments have a clear purpose. It is the student, supported by the family, who is responsible for completing the assignment.

Student Record-Keeping

Self-recording is a premier tool for changing behavior. Want to change your eating behavior? No self-respecting diet program leaves out self-recording. The first step is to record how much you are really eating. The same is true for athletic programs. Athletes who want to improve a skill, or keep a skill at a high level, keep track of their own performance. Want to boost a student's academic morale? Have that student record his or her achievements after practice sessions for a visible record of his or her progress.

When students record the amount of time that they are studying, the message given to them is that it is effort that counts. Yes, the product is important too, but the way that we learn to produce quality work is through effort, spending time in practice.

Recording time spent on homework is not only an indication that children are spending the minimum required times studying, but it is also a learning tool. By the end of sixth grade, students will have learned how to allocate their time. They will know how long it usually takes them to read an average length book, how long it takes for them to do the required research for a paper, what subjects they need to spend more time practicing, and they will have seen, over and over, the relationship between effort and achievement.

When children see that their effort is producing results, the result is excitement and motivation. It is far easier to see the relationship between effort and results when children are recording their time spent (effort) and then seeing improvement in subject areas they have been practicing. The system makes this relationship clear.

If our students record their study times and indicate what it is that they have been working on, the result is also a rich source of data for teachers and parents. Teachers and parents can do some joint problem solving when they see a student struggling overtime in a subject area. The record will be there: "My student is spending all of his time on math and is becoming discouraged." Is it time to intervene? Change tactics? Provide some tutoring? At any point in the academic year parents, students, and teachers have available clear information about individual study patterns and, best of all, teachers don't have to gather the data; the students do it on their own, with their parents support.

Children react in many different ways to what they view as "failure." For example, one child may demonstrate the same ability in mathematics as another child (they may have similar math scores on aptitude tests and achievement tests). However, when these children see a lot of mistakes on a math paper one child may say, "Guess I need to study harder." The other child may say, "I'm no good in math." The next time they face a math test, guess which child does better? Of course, the one who said, "Oops, I need to study more."

We want to encourage our children to persevere even when tasks are challenging. They will, if the messages we give them stress the value of effort.

"Mistakes show us how to improve."

"Remember when you learned to ride your bicycle? You kept practicing until you did it."

"I'm really proud of your effort."

Accountability

Homework is most effective when students are held responsible for studying and completing assignments. Self-recording leads naturally to a system of accountability that promotes effort. In the proposed system, students are required to record the time that they spend on homework and parents are asked to sign or initial the homework assignments and the time spent on the weekly homework form. Students add the number of minutes spent each week. If the number of minutes is sufficient, the student gets credit for homework. Under this system very objective criteria can be set up for a homework grade or evaluation. For example, every child will be required to spend a specified amount of time on approved homework projects in order to receive a "satisfactory" grade. An "unsatisfactory" evaluation is the result of minimum times not met. An "excellent" evaluation is the result of exceeding the maximum amount of time on learning tasks. Suzanne Brady uses pluses and minuses to indicate whether time spent was satisfactory or unsatisfactory. The recording is simple: Minimum time taken? (+) Time not taken? (-) Time taken and exceptional quality?

(++) Students love this system. They can tally their pluses any time to see how they are doing. Students know how many pluses they need by the end of the quarter for a satisfactory or excellent homework grade and they can work for the grade they want. Consequences and choices are clear. Success is possible for every student regardless of current skill level.

Asking parents to validate the daily times spent each week encourages consistent study. An "excellent" or "satisfactory" evaluation on a student's report card can be reinforced by a family celebration. "I'm proud of your homework grade. All that effort deserves a family night out!"

Some homework assignments (primarily teacher-assigned) will be given evaluations or grades separate from the overall "homework" grade. These will be reflected under appropriate subject area headings on the report card or in the student's portfolio. However, especially at the elementary level, it is important to hold students accountable for time spent in study. If we hold students accountable for time, they get this message: "My parents (guardians) and the school think that time spent studying is important. They are united on this. Guess I have to turn off the television."

As studies of recent immigrants to North America have so vividly illustrated, family customs can support effective study skills. Students in our current system of education do demonstrate high levels of achievement in a variety of different schools under a variety of different conditions. Families of high risk children have successfully helped their children develop study skills through family programs that require a daily amount of study. However, the most effective way to achieve a high level of study skills for all children is through a partnership with the school; parents and teachers support the same requirements and hold students accountable for meeting them.

Feedback

The type of feedback and reinforcement that students receive for doing homework will vary with each classroom and each family. To be effective, homework must be commented upon by the teacher. This is the most powerful reinforcer. Specific comments from the teacher have the same positive effect as individual attention.

A systematic homework program that reinforces strong study skills, can help students begin to view study as intrinsically rewarding. Increased self-confidence, and pride in growing competencies are the outcome of studying. It helps students view studying as something they want to do because they want to learn. However, many high school and junior high students still need support from home in the form of established study hours, help when requested, and encouragement for effort. Older students may require encouragement to establish long-term goals. Short-range goals such as buying a car, paying for insurance, or acquiring material possessions, may require long hours at unskilled jobs. For many of today's students these short-range goals interfere with study time and quality school work. More than three times as many American as Asian students have after-school jobs, seventy-four percent versus twenty-one percent (Stevenson, Chen and Lee, 1992).

Unless we, as parents and teachers, send a clear message that it is important for upper level students to devote wholehearted time to study, our children are going to have difficulty achieving their long-range goals.

Choice

Teacher assignments are the first priority. However, the element of choice creates participation ("buy-in") from students. Student choice may be developed by giving students report topic options, or choice of methods to achieve a goal.

Another form of choice is the following requirement: When students do not have a formal teacher-assigned task or project to work on, they are responsible for choosing a task or area of study. This is an important independence builder. It gives the message: "The life of your mind is important and you are responsible for making decisions about how to allocate your time."

Students who live with this message learn to take responsibility for developing their talents and skills. How many parents have heard their children say, "I'm bored," when the television is turned off on a rainy day? The same children can think up hundreds of absorbing things to do with a little practice and they won't miss the television when it is turned off on a regular basis.

When students are required to come up with projects that stimulate their interest and talent, these students learn how to become self-directed. Ultimately the ability to be independent will enable them to succeed in the world that exists outside of the school yard. It is our job as parents and teachers to help develop the ability to be independent thinkers and capable decision-makers. We can do this by requiring independent work as our children progress through the school system.

Routine

Our goal is to develop effective study habits. A "habit" is a way of acting that becomes fixed through repetition. If our students repeat a behavior long enough, like studying every school night, study will become a habit.

In many countries studying is such a customary and widespread activity that it is the social norm. Children in these countries do not feel that studying is stressful. When faced with tasks that are challenging, many Asian and European students proceed with more confidence than North American students, because they have acquired the study habits that are the key to achievement.

If students are required to study at least from Monday through Thursday for a portion of every evening, studying will become the accepted routine. Quality assignments and self-choice will make this routine rewarding and exciting. When schools can announce, "Every student at our school is required to spend a minimum amount of time each night from Monday through Thursday studying," then we will have begun a cultural revolution in our communities.

It is important to keep in mind that our North American culture values creativity. This system requires all students to spend time studying. Some critics may say that it therefore encourages uniformity. In actuality, the opposite is true. True creativity requires effort and a strong knowledge base. This system enhances both. Because this system requires self-choice, it also encourages the independence and motivation that foster creativity. Finally, creativity requires the confidence to take risks, to try solutions that are unique. If we value each student's chosen ways of learning, over a period of years we will build this confidence.

Weekly Communication

Communication is the keystone of this system. Without it, the system collapses. When homework assignments are communicated to students and their families in a routine way, support and completion of homework are enhanced. At the elementary school level, communication weekly is desirable. When families live with the system, over time, they learn to expect assignments on a regular basis. It becomes easier to establish family schedules that accommodate study. It becomes difficult for students to say, "I didn't know about that assignment," when for months, assignments have been coming home on identical forms every week on the same day of each week. Parents feel involved when they know what the weekly school requirements are for their students. "No more, 'But I don't have any homework tonight.' (Every student has homework Monday through Thursday.) No more, 'I'll do it tomorrow.' (All students have a known minimum time per night to spend on home learning.) No more, 'The other kids don't have to do any homework. Why should I?' (See the above two answers.) No more, 'I forgot I had any.' Pretty hard to 'forget' when it's automatic. This one might be believable for the first week. After that, no way!" (Richard Pierce, Sandburg Homework Committee)

Each week, if a homework log is used, a tally of time spent on study is available. In a quick glance teachers have available to them a record of how much time was used on what activities.

Both teachers and parents are alerted on a weekly basis to those students who are struggling with assignments, or students who are not spending time studying. Alternatives and suggestions can be made weekly, rather than letting large lapses of time go by before parent-teacher communication is achieved.

This kind of weekly communication is simple but powerful. For example, a note on the weekly homework form written by the teacher might say, "I can see that Joe is spending a lot of time on math problems and he indicates that he is frustrated. Let's try this: . . ." Solutions can take many forms; "Joe" can be tutored by a student who is skilled, his parent or guardian can use a set of games or classroom materials to work with him, the teacher can recommend individual time with a specialist, etc. Problems can be spotted before they create unnecessary discouragement.

Teachers can also see at a glance which students finish work quickly and what kind of additional work is undertaken. With this information, teachers can more easily act as advisors and mentors for motivated students. Capable students learn that they have to take responsibility for their scholarship. At the same time, teachers receive the information they need to guide individual students and support their growing talents.

Parents also have access to the routine weekly form to communicate with the teacher. ("My child is having difficulty with this week's assignment. Any suggestions?")

When the method of communication is routine, easy to access, and two-way, collaborative problem-solving can become a true collaboration among teachers, students and parents.

Chapter 10

Implementation

The homework system is based on time. The primary goal is to reinforce and enhance effort. The result could be an enormous culture change, but we have our work cut out for us. A decade of heightened emphasis in the United States on science and math has had little influence on achievement or parental attitudes. American elementary school children in 1990 lagged behind their Chinese and Japanese counterparts to as great a degree as they did in 1980 (Stevenson, Chen, and Lee, 1992). After a decade of reform attempts American students' achievement remains low. Despite publicity about the need for reform, for upgrading standards, and for assigning more and better quality homework, the parents in the Stevenson study were no more enthusiastic about instituting changes in 1990 than they had been in 1980 or 1984. In view of these attitudes, and the continued poor performance of our students, we have an uphill climb ahead of us to increase support for change. The most powerful force for change is shared information. As "school people" we need to gather groups of parents, teachers and administrators together to exchange information about homework and then simply get started.

> "This may seem like work for parents at first. However, once the routine is set up parents see the value of keeping in touch with what their children are learning and doing at school." —M. REIMER, TEACHER, CHARLIE LAKE ELEMENTARY

Information-gathering and discussion among teachers, students and parents is the most time-consuming part of getting a homework system started. Once you set the routine in place it saves time, gets results, and is more fun for all involved.

Is the Brady System in use?

Three schools are currently using variations of the Brady System: two in the United States, and one in Canada. Each school has adopted the basic features of the program with revisions that reflect the values of their school community. Several more schools are already requesting information about the system.

The road to implementation of new homework policies at these schools was heady and exciting, but not without a certain share of bumps. At one school the homework system was introduced by a parent, at another school the system was introduced by an administrator, and at another the program was introduced by a teacher and staff member.

At Carl Sandburg, a school in Washington state, the focus on homework was initiated by parents via a "Dads' group" meeting. The dads at the meeting were not satisfied with the amount of homework that their children were bringing home, nor were they satisfied with the quality of work their children were producing. Armed with an outline of the Brady System, and fortified with numerous articles on homework, the parents proposed a change. The initial reaction by a few concerned teachers was resistance. Are a few pushy parents trying to control curriculum? Are parents trying to control what is assigned for homework? We're already overloaded with paperwork; is this system going to require more? The homework plan received a hearing primarily because a teacher, acting as a staff representative, spent many hours with the homework committee, reading and discussing information, conveying information back to the staff, and then promoting changes during staff meetings.

At Charlie Lake Elementary School in B.C., the Vice-Principal responded to staff concern and frustration regarding homework by providing information and arranging time for teachers to study and discuss homework research. Teachers at this school engaged in open discussion and debate. As a result, the staff cheerfully and enthusiastically took up the homework banner and were met with initial resistance by a few concerned parents. "Is the school trying to interfere in our family life? Are we being told what to do in our time at home?" Discussion meetings at this school site were held to provide parents with information about the system. Parents were also given the opportunity to discuss the system and to voice questions and concerns.

When parents understood the reasons for building a homework partnership, and were given discussion opportunities with school staff, the road was cleared for collaboration.

In Monterey, at Monte Vista Elementary, a teacher, who also happens to be the originator of the homework program, was supported enthusiastically by parents but met initial resistance from colleagues: "I already have my own system, thank you." At this school, colleagues observed the changes in student study habits generated by the homework system and individually sought more information about it. Gradually, more staff members began to implement it. Comments from staff members such as, "I finally have a handle on homework!" or "Students used to turn in homework in dribbles and drabs, now they're turning in their work on time. I feel more in control," continue to draw in new practitioners of the homework partnership system.

In all three schools positive changes resulted from shared information and opportunities for open discussion. Members of the school community who had access to accurate, up-to-date information and discussion opportunities developed working partnerships regarding homework. Initial resistance came from groups who had not been included in the information and discussion stages. When all groups (teachers, parents, administrators, students) perceived themselves to be part of the decision-making process, a great deal of energy and goodwill was released and innovative homework systems, with buy-in from all partners in the education process, was the result. These school communities relied upon information and community input to build shared visions and action plans.

> "I was reluctant to do this initially. I always believed if my students worked hard at school they should have free time at home. But after using this system my kids are doing so much better in math and reading. The parents like it and it provides important opportunities for us to communicate. I'm for it." —CARLA VENNES, TEACHER, CHARLIE LAKE ELEMENTARY

At Charlie Lake Elementary School in British Columbia, the homework system is reinforced with an "incentive package." Students who fulfill their time requirements and exhibit cooperative behavior in class earn the privilege of participating in "Charger Days." (The school mascot is a charging rhino.) Sought-after activities and projects are sponsored by parents and staff. All students have the ability and resources to participate if they choose to put forth the effort. Parents at this school love the way that students are being reinforced for effort, instead of being penalized for what they "fail" to do.

The process at these schools is not complete. In order to continue to be effective as a homework policy, two basic activities need to receive regular attention: continued, shared access to information, and open discussion. Incoming groups, like kindergarten families, families new to the school, and new staff members, will need access to information and opportunities for discussion if the system is to continue to function well. Outgoing groups, students who are moving on to junior high or middle schools, will require continued access to information about school homework policies, and opportunities for discussion in order to build upon the gains made at the elementary school level.

Are examples available of existing homework policies that are based on the Brady System?

The Appendix includes a copy of the Sandburg Homework Policy adopted by an elementary school in Washington (Appendix B), and the Charlie Lake Homework Policy (Appendix D) adopted by an elementary school in British Columbia. The policy statements are brief, but they incorporate the major components of the Brady System.

The Sandburg homework philosophy and definition of homework cited below are examples of collaborative efforts among parents, students, and teachers.

SANDBURG HOMEWORK PHILOSOPHY

"Parent-teacher-student interaction and partnerships are strengthened and enhanced with a homework system that reinforces effort, responsibility, and motivation.

For the student, learning is a process of active participation and discovery. As an extension of school, homework serves to develop methods and habits to empower students to become independent and resourceful learners.

Effective homework policies recognize teachers as professionals. The Sandburg policy does not dictate curriculum but serves as an extension of the classroom, and a means to develop the unique interests of individual students. Students practice and refine skills learned in class, prepare for new material, expand on class activities by applying learning to situations outside the classroom, and stimulate creativity through activities requiring original expression.

Effective homework policies also recognize that parents are actively involved in their child's education and social interaction. Homework serves as a "dialogue" between home and school as well as a process to encourage and reinforce positive parent involvement.

Homework for students from kindergarten through third grade should be designed to foster success, self-esteem, and routine study habits. Effort is emphasized and reinforced.

Homework for students from grades four through six should enhance specific academic skills plus independence and self-discipline.

At all levels, homework should be designed to promote personal interest in learning and discovery."

—SANDBURG HOMEWORK COMMITTEE

Sandburg Homework Definition

> Homework is any mental activity, creative, technical, or aesthetic, accomplished outside of the classroom environment, that improves a child's understanding and ability to function successfully within the world.
>
> —SANDBURG HOMEWORK COMMITTEE

Teachers have the freedom to assign the work that is deemed valuable. Individual family values are also respected by including the element of student choice. The committee agreed that provisions for consistent minimum time requirements, accountability, and a system for communication with the home, are necessities. The responsibility for completing homework is seen as the responsibility of the student. The system, by linking families with the school, provided a way for Sandburg families to learn how to build study habits. Parents and teachers are seeing concrete results.

What procedures did the Sandburg community follow to implement a new homework policy?

Homework is an emotional issue for many parents and teachers because it touches upon personal beliefs. ("My children are not getting enough homework," "My children are getting too much homework," "Parents don't support my classroom homework assignments," "Are my values going to be respected?" etc.) The homework issue can serve as a concrete example of how a focus on information and community input can be the basis for improvement. Information and dialogue enable parents and teachers to step out of the cycle of blame and take the first strides forward. Information helps us to choose the appropriate steps. Formal means of gathering input from all who will be affected by decisions increases participation.

The following are steps that occurred at Sandburg in the Lake Washington School District that led to the adoption of a Brady-based homework policy:

STEP 1

Parents met to discuss school issues. Homework was targeted as a focal parent concern. (An example of a focus on goals and values at individual school sites.)

STEP 2

Parents and teachers agreed to form a homework committee. Input was solicited through a school-wide questionnaire and open meetings. (Procedures for discussion of school issues and gathering information can become a way of life at local school sites.)

STEP 3

Research was collected and discussed. Information-gathering responsibility was delegated to committee members. The Office of the Superintendent may provide invaluable aid collecting information in many school districts. Because central administrators have a more flexible working schedule and greater access to resources than do teachers and staff, they can be very effective in responding to staff requests for information.

STEP 4

Committee members agreed on a homework philosophy and reached consensus on the components to be included in the homework proposal.

STEP 5

The Homework Committee presented conclusions to the staff. The committee's plan was adopted unanimously after lively discussion and debate and resulting revisions.

STEP 6

The homework system was presented to parents via flyers and the school handbook. Homework Committee meetings were open to all interested parties.

STEP 7

The homework committee continues to provide information and gather input from parents and teachers in order to assess how well the system is working. A survey was conducted and results published.

In the future, attention will be paid to entry groups, including kindergarten families and families new to the school. Exit groups (sixth grade families) will discuss ways to capitalize on the gains made in elementary school as their children enter junior and senior high.

The process works; information and shared values can result in measurable changes and greater academic achievement for our students. Homework is not a teaching problem, it is a partnership problem. Homework is a starting place for convincing parents and teachers that they can build partnerships, and that cultural changes can occur in our communities through access to information. The process of building an information base and developing shared goals can be applied to any school governance or curriculum issue.

Did the homework system affect children's attitudes about homework?

The best assessment of any program change is, how does this (program, policy, method) affect our children's desire to learn? In this regard the comments of the parents, teachers, and students who adopted the Brady System are the most valuable measures of success.

A follow-up survey at Sandburg was conducted six months after the new policy went into effect. The results from the parent poll were extremely positive: seventy-four percent of the parents felt that the new system had improved their children's attitude toward homework, twenty-one percent had not seen a change in attitude. In a few classrooms students were not required to record their work nor were parents asked to sign time sheets. Students were also not held accountable for selecting independent projects after teacher assigned work was completed. These classrooms did not seem to benefit from improved attitudes toward homework.

Eighty-three percent of the parents indicated that the new homework policy was more effective in generating student involvement, and eighty-four percent indicated that their children were becoming more responsible for their work. None of the responses indicated a negative effect.

At Charlie Lake Elementary, the results of the follow-up survey were as follows:

	Agree	**Disagree**
Effective in generating student involvement	91%	9%
Effective in promoting parent involvement	92%	8%
Improved child's attitude toward homework	63%	37%
Helps student take responsibility for homework	75%	25%
Reduced conflict at home regarding homework	70%	30%
Increased communication with teacher	66%	34%

Survey results indicate that positive changes occurred within an astonishingly short time. These schools had been using the system for less than one school year. The potential for long-range improvement of student attitude toward homework and involvement in homework activities is real.

What are the key elements for implementing homework policy revisions at school sites?

When routine channels exist for discussion of school issues, positive change can be generated by dialogue between staff and parents. It is helpful when decision-making councils include representatives from all school subgroups (faculty, staff, parents and students).

If all parties, students, teachers, and parents, feel that they have been included in decision-making processes, greater support for the decision ensues. Mutual respect is the underlying philosophy governing the Brady System. Goals are clearly communicated, teacher professionalism is maintained, diverse family values are acknowledged by the school. The key procedures for implementing the system, discussion and shared information, are also based on mutual respect. If the goal is to form working partnerships, the following procedures are essential:

- Formal input concerning proposed changes is gathered from all those who are affected by decisions.
- Collaborative decision-making procedures are utilized by the school council and staff.

- Pertinent information is made available to all concerned and changes are accompanied by supporting arguments and summaries of school community input.

Dialogue is necessary for wide-ranging changes to take place. To illustrate, the following staff communication occurred at Sandburg through the school telemail:

FROM: HOMEWORK COMMITTEE STAFF LIAISON
TO: SANDBURG STAFF

"As you all know, I have been working with the homework committee to review our policy. I need some help from you since I am always being asked by the committee for your opinions. I never speak for all of you and lately I've had to say 'I don't know,' a lot. I think it's time to help the committee out by giving some input. We don't want them to go to a lot of work if we are not going to buy into it. The committee does realize that teacher buy-in is of utmost importance and they do not want to try to tell us what to do in our classrooms!

"Research seems to show that most homework policies like ours describe goals but leave out the process for achieving the goals. Homework can improve achievement and it has even more impact when teachers comment on it or grade it. Based on these findings and several more that I can make available to you, the committee members seem to feel that homework is a parent problem, not a teacher problem. They do not want to add to our workload. (My opinion: If the research indicates that teacher involvement is important, we need to listen, especially if even minimal support increases achievement.) They are leaning towards time commitment (research backs time as a big factor, especially since most students spend more time watching television than doing homework). The committee seems to be heading toward parent involvement with our support. For instance: let's say a sixth grade student is required to do an hour of homework per night. I give an assignment to the whole class just as I do now. One student gets it done the first night. His parents would then say, "Good, now what are you going to do for the rest of your homework time?" We plan on having ideas to help with this time. Say another student uses all the time to do the assignments that I have given. When both students bring in their forms (and we haven't exactly decided on this yet, we are leaning toward something that hooks in with our calendars) and the first student has done work that is acceptable to me and to parents (definitely not sports) then I give both credit for homework. What do you think? Let me know."

BARBARA WOOLSEY (SANDBURG TEACHER)

The return answers were varied. Several teachers took the time to answer on the telemail.

FROM: SANDBURG STAFF

TO: HOMEWORK COMMITTEE STAFF LIAISON

"I have some opinions about homework which are based on my observations of different communities over the years.

The students who benefit most from homework are those whose parents actually look at their calendars, their completed work, and their corrected or graded final results. Parents who just say, 'Do you have any homework?' and then leave it to the student to think it over and decide whether or not they should do homework, watch television, or go outside, frequently do not get completely honest answers. These students may conveniently forget about the work, or leave it at school.

Parents who schedule a quiet homework, reading, or study time each day have students who do the very best. I had a boy two years ago who was two years behind in reading and language. His mom decided school work was going to be a number one priority until he was doing the best he could. She checked his calendar daily, was available to help when he needed it and held him to a standard that was realistic but higher than he had set for himself. It was amazing how much he improved. He began to take pride in his work and almost enjoyed it.

Teachers, like students, live up to the expectations of the community. Our students watch an incredible amount of television. It's sort of a hidden fact that no one really admits to. I think the amount of homework had been pulled down by a lack of support. If we get lots of students who don't complete assignments, or if we get lots of notes asking us to excuse students from assignments, we are gradually discouraged from assigning very much homework. Also, if one-third of a class doesn't complete an assignment, it slows down the whole group's progress. Homework is largely practice, and practice is essential for mastery. In elementary school where we introduce the basic skills, a once over lightly won't do the job.

Research shows that time on task is a major factor in mastery learning. We need a school culture that supports academic achievement. This is not to say that social skills, arts, music, P.E., drama, health education, safety, self-esteem, crafts, and vocational skills aren't vital to a child's development and shouldn't be part of what we do at school; they make school meaningful and enrich a child's entire life. We do have to remember that the only place students get the basic academic skills is in school and teachers need the academics to be supported at home every day—not just sometimes, or when there is nothing else going on. Sports, scouts, church youth groups and all the other wonderful activities our students have are great, but they are not substitutes for the academic practice that homework provides.

Where does the American education system seem to be falling behind, compared to many other countries in the developed world? I read that not enough of our high school graduates have mastered the basic skills. It really isn't that the schools don't teach the skills. I'm afraid the students don't get enough chance to practice.

Now, lots of luck in condensing this so the committee can process it!

NANCY MENDENHALL (SANDBURG TEACHER)

Telemail communication provided fodder for lively debate. Eventually the entire staff gathered as a group and voted to use the homework system. Each school will have its own unique way to discuss issues. The telemail at Sandburg and the Dads' Group meetings were the initial "gathering places."

The search for solutions was productive in the positive atmosphere. It is difficult for either children or adults to be creative and productive in an atmosphere of criticism and blame. School partnerships thrive on mutual respect.

Is the Brady System appropriate for junior and senior high students?

No. It should not be necessary. A student starting in kindergarten and living with this system will be well served. By sixth grade it is expected that these students will be self-motivated and thus complete assignments without undue prompting or nagging. Study will simply have become a way of life. The first steps toward self-discipline will have been practiced and self-esteem enhanced along the way.

However, middle school students will also benefit from a coordinated school-wide homework policy. Minimum homework times are still helpful in maintaining habits, especially for those students who have not benefited from a coordinated plan at the elementary level. Because middle school students see more than one teacher for instruction, a homework calendar will require a different format. A school homework calendar with space for assignments or a daily planner should be a requirement for all students.

Formal minimum homework time requirements and self-recording of homework time are appropriate for students whose grades and homework completion fall below acceptable levels. Homework information and counseling for families whose students obtain failing grades can help families organize study time more effectively.

Even though the homework policy takes a different form at older grade levels, older students still need parents to support their academic goals. Parents can give their high school and junior high school sons and daughters an enormous boost by requiring minimum study times and specifying the time of evening that study should be terminated. Two hours of study a night for junior high students still leaves plenty of time for after school sports and activities. For high school students, whether in an academic or vocational program, a minimum of ten hours of study a week is recommended. These minimum times should not interfere with an adolescent's need for a good night's sleep but they are very likely to interfere with television time and with long work hours at part-time jobs.

At junior and senior high a homework partnership is still a necessity. Policies should be provided in written form, revised and evaluated on a periodic basis and, above all, should be the result of a collaboration among teachers. Periodic evaluation should include input from the school community regarding homework.

Syllabi for each course at the junior high and high school level listing class requirements can be an invaluable aid to students in planning efficient use of study time. Teachers will find them invaluable in assessing the school-wide quantity and variety of assignments and for coordinating assignments across subject matter. Staff will find syllabi handy in answering the following questions:

- Are students at this school given enough opportunities to develop written expression?
- Are students at this school given enough opportunities to develop research skills?
- Are students required to edit and revise their work on a routine basis?

After-school activities should include computer time at home or in the school computer lab using word processors and spelling programs to edit written work. School libraries are ideal meeting places for peer tutoring and study groups.

A modified version of the Brady System will help older students who are having academic difficulties get back on track. For students who are not maintaining a passing grade point average, a homework program can be an automatic school requirement. Programs such as the Academic Skills Workshop (Quackenbush, 1989) provide a model for helping students and their parents cope with academic tasks. Students are required to spend time studying on a regular basis from Monday through Thursday and they are given help in breaking up assignments into manageable parts so that they can take the first steps without being overwhelmed. A parent or guardian is asked to sign a weekly homework form for these students validating minimum times spent in study. Fulfillment of minimum time requirements may be deemed necessary for students who have a failing grade in a class in order to participate in sports and school activities.

Mandatory tutoring and after-school study halls for students failing one or more subjects can be developed as a routine school service. Many schools offer before and after school tutoring and participate in "homework hotlines," providing students with numbers to call to check on assignments.

High expectations and similar levels of homework opportunities should be made available for vocational courses as well as for college preparatory courses. Often, students enrolled in vocational courses are required to do considerably less homework than their academic track peers (Murphy & Decker, 1990). This pattern is based on faulty assumptions. Students who are allowed fewer opportunities to practice and develop skills are disadvantaged by the educational process (Oakes, 1985).

What is the origin of the Brady System?

This homework system evolved as part of a teaching approach that was designed to help students develop an active role in their learning. Suzanne Brady compares her homework system to a builder's scaffold. The framework supports students as they develop study techniques and thinking skills that lead to independent learning. "When the building is sturdy, the scaffold is no longer needed." Suzanne Brady discusses the life of her classroom in the book, *Mindful of Others* (Brady & Jacobs, 1994).

The co-author of *Homework: Bridging the Gap* experienced the system first hand when her fifth grade son became a member of Suzanne's classroom. The positive change in her son's attitude toward homework was startling. The absence of parental nagging was appreciated by all family members. Under the Brady System, the parent knew what was happening in the classroom, what was expected by the teacher, exactly how much the child was studying, and she gained new appreciation for her child's interests. The bite of anxiety simply disappeared for parent and student alike.

The old after dinner routine . . .

"You have to do your homework!"

"I don't have any!"

"Well, do something besides watch television."

"I finished, why should I work on school work?"

. . . was replaced by . . .

"What's up for homework?

"I finished my math and the wagon train diary. I think I'm going to build a model of a Conestoga for extra credit."

. . . or . . .

"I'm all caught up, I'm going to read."

. . . or . . .

"I have time to finish my rocket model."

The conversation on some nights sounded like the following:

"How about writing those thank-you notes to your grandparents? It can count as homework."

"OK, after I finish my book report."

Suzanne found that this quiet revolution in one home, happened over and over in other homes as her students adjusted to the new way of thinking about homework. Busy families found that the clear expectation, consistency and organization took the stress out of homework time. Like other public elementary schools in North America, some of the families of her students were struggling with problems involving economic survival, addictions to drugs and alcohol, and emotional instability. She found that the homework system was especially important when, for numerous reasons, her students lacked support from home. Even students living in chaotic conditions were able to complete more homework on their own.

Students who couldn't study at home worked in the library or at a friend's house in order to spend the required minutes in study. Suzanne assigned homework buddies at the beginning of the year so that students could help each other in case of an absence from school or difficulties with homework assignments. At different times, school librarians, custodians, older siblings, and counselors volunteered to sign homework logs to indicate that the time a student spent was valid. Peers are often recruited as tutors, and homework labs and homework hotlines have appeared in schools to encourage those students who are struggling. These brave young people who are struggling on their own are finding their persistence rewarded.

Conclusion

What the authors have tried to do with this text is to provide the basic material needed to bring about changes in our homework systems; information and specific solutions, so that there is material for discussion and debate. When changes in our system of education are accompanied by clearly stated justifications, greater acceptance ensues. When solutions are generated and formally adopted by the people who will be affected by decisions, participation increases.

The need for better study habits has been identified by the people at the forefront: our teachers and students. It is time to support them. The challenge is this: how do we assure that our children have the skills they need to lead productive and satisfying lives? How do we promote high standards without discouraging our students? A school-wide homework system can provide the necessary scaffold as students develop the skills they need to face difficult tasks. When study becomes a habit, the scaffold is no longer necessary. By requiring effort, by enabling students to make independent choices, by allowing students the opportunity to learn in ways that encourage their interests and talents, we set them free.

We are a diverse culture that values independence and creativity. Some families enjoy literature, or the rhythm of the spoken word. Others encourage their child's interest in science and technology. Some children love to write, others love the logic of math. What we need to do is identify our students' strengths and show them how they can pursue their goals. The homework system that we propose respects cultural differences; it opens doors by encouraging every family's unique values.

Effective writing takes practice to achieve. So does logical thinking. The road to accomplishment is not easy, it requires effort, but we also want our children to know how satisfying the journey can be. As adults, many of us have forgotten how much fun learning is, and we forget to share the joy of it with our children. If we show them how to stick their toes into the water, pretty soon they're swimming and loving it.

Techniques for tackling tough problems are more important than the actual product. If we give our students a good foundation in study skills and, at the same time, encourage their curiosity, they will realize their dreams. A homework partnership can build the bridge for them.

—KAY L. MORISON & SUZANNE BRADY

Appendices

Appendix A: Sandburg Homework Questionnaire

Appendix B: Sandburg Homework Policy

Appendix C: Sandburg Follow-up Survey

Appendix D: Charlie Lake Homework Summary

APPENDIX A

SANDBURG HOMEWORK QUESTIONNAIRE

Within the Restructuring process, we are reviewing the current Carl Sandburg Homework Policy. Your input will help us understand the homework needs of teachers, parents, and students. (Please return completed questionnaires to the tables in the halls outside your child's classroom.)

---

1. What grade levels are your children attending at Sandburg?

K 1 2 3 4 5 6

2. Are you familiar with the 1991-1992 homework policy?

Yes No

3. How would you change the following area of the current Sandburg Homework Policy?:

A. Amount of time	More	Less	Same
B. Amount of Homework	More	Less	Same
C. Content Tied to class work	More	Less	Same
D. Student responsibility	More	Less	Same
E. Parent responsibility	More	Less	Same
F. Teacher responsibility	More	Less	Same
G. Consistency within grade level	More	Less	Same
H. Consistency from grade to grade	More	Less	Same

I. Other: ____________________

4. Do you feel there are benefits to homework? Yes No
Explain:____

5. Is the current policy serving your child's needs?
Yes No

6. Has the current policy been well-communicated to parents? Yes No

7. What is the average number of minutes that your child spends on homework from Monday through Thursday?
0-15 15-30 30-60 60-90 More than 90

8. To what extent do you become involved in your child's homework?

A. Homework is not done at home.

B. I get them started and am available to answer questions.

C. We do it together.

D. I end up doing most of the homework.

E. Child sits down without direction and completes homework.

F. Other: ________________________________
____

9. Are there home activities that you would like to see credited as homework? Yes No
Please List:____
____

10. How much homework should be given by grade?

Grade level	Days per week	Minutes per day
Kindergarten	____________	____________
First	____________	____________
Second	____________	____________
Third	____________	____________
Fourth	____________	____________
Fifth	____________	____________
Sixth	____________	____________

11. Would you support a policy that requires parent participation on a regular basis? Yes No

12. Should homework be an activity evaluated on the report card? Yes No

13. Would you be interested in homework assistance programs such as study halls, peer tutoring, homework hot lines, etc. ? Yes No

14. Would you prefer homework assistance programs

A. during the school day B. after school C. not at all

15. Additional Comments? (Please write them on the back)

Thank you for your participation!

If you would like to participate in an on-going review of the homework policy, please write your name and number on the back of this questionnaire.

THE HOMEWORK COMMITTEE

Sandburg Questionnaire Results

A large number of parents participated in the survey, indicating a high degree of interest in the subject of homework. A number of parents who responded had two or three children enrolled in the school. The 202 responses reflects the number of students represented. The participating parents were spread evenly among the six grade levels. An average of thirty parents from each grade (Grades 1-6) responded as well as twenty-one kindergarten parents, seventeen teachers, and forty-one students.

The survey was conducted during parent-teacher conferences in order to maximize the number of responses. The current policy was posted at each classroom station so all parents were provided an opportunity to review the existing policy. The majority of parents who completed the survey were familiar with the existing policy.

The following are highlights and generalizations taken from the data:

1. Homework is perceived to be beneficial and desirable.
2. The homework program is an important part of school and should have appropriate emphasis.
3. Time spent on homework should increase as grade level increases.
4. Minimum homework time requirements should be the same among all classrooms at any grade level.

5. Sandburg homework goals and policy should be clearly communicated to parents.

6. A successful homework program will involve participation by both parents and teachers.

7. Responsibility for the completion of homework should lie with the students with support by parents. Most respondents indicated that increased student responsibility for completion of homework was desirable.

8. Most Sandburg students currently study between 0-30 minutes per day.

9. Most parents tend to believe that there should be four days of homework a week.

10. A tendency toward the following minutes per day to be devoted to homework was as follows:

Kindergarten	=	0-10 minutes
Grade 1	=	10-20 minutes
Grade 2	=	20-25 minutes
Grade 3	=	20-30 minutes
Grade 4	=	30 minutes
Grade 5	=	30-50 minutes
Grade 6	=	30-60 minutes

11. Most respondents indicated support for the idea of a homework grade.

12. Although there was not a clear consensus on the benefits of a homework assistance program, the preference expressed was that homework assistance take place during school hours.

Appendix B
Sandburg Homework Policy

PARENTS. . . . HERE IT IS!

THE NEW AND IMPROVED SANDBURG HOMEWORK SYSTEM!

It's easy, simple, and straightforward AND it makes the kids responsible. After all, it is their homework!

No more, "But I don't have any homework tonight."
(Every Sandburg student has homework Monday through Thursday.)

No more, "I'll do it tomorrow."
(All students have a known minimum time per night to spend on home learning.)

No more, "The other kids don't have to do any homework. Why should I?"
(See the above two answers.)

No more, "I forgot I had any."
(Pretty hard to "forget" when it's automatic. This one might be believable for the first week. After that, no way!)

All you conscientious parents have to do is provide a

place for your children to do their homework and be aware of how much time they spend doing it. Throw in a little encouragement and love and your child is on the way to a lifelong habit of accomplishment and success.

SANDBURG HOMEWORK COMMITTEE

1992-1993 Sandburg Homework Policy

The Sandburg Homework Philosophy and Policy is derived from Sandburg teacher recommendations, the Sandburg Parent Homework Survey, and conclusions based on reviews of homework research.

POLICY =

'91-'92 policy	+	Minimum time requirements (Derived from the Sandburg survey and homework research)	+	Accountability (survey and research)	+	Method for implementing (Classroom Teachers)

Common values expressed in the 1992 Sandburg homework survey were: the need for parent-teacher partnerships regarding homework, increased student responsibility for homework and the desire to protect teacher autonomy. The vision of the community was supported by a thorough review of homework research. Public school students simply are not doing enough homework. A planned, long-range homework policy that calls for parent-teacher communication can help students develop the study habits that they need to lead productive lives and, at the same time enhance their lifelong love of learning. This homework policy specifies consistent grade level time requirements, provisions for parent support, and a method for promoting accountability.

I. Sandburg Homework Philosophy

Parent-teacher-student interaction and partnerships are strengthened and enhanced with a homework system that reinforces effort, responsibility, and motivation.

For the student, learning is a process of active participation and discovery. As an extension to school, homework serves to develop methods and habits to empower students to become independent and resourceful learners.

Effective homework policies recognize teachers as professionals. The Sandburg policy does not dictate curriculum but serves as an extension of the classroom and a means to develop the unique interests of individual students. Students practice and refine skills learned in class, prepare for new material, expand on class activities by applying learning to situations outside the classroom, and stimulate creativity through activities requiring original expression.

Effective homework policies also recognize that parents are actively involved in their child's education and social interaction. Homework serves as a "dialogue" between home and school as well as a process to encourage and reinforce positive parent involvement.

Homework for students from kindergarten through third grade should be designed to foster success, self-esteem, and routine study habits. Effort is emphasized and reinforced.

Homework for students from grades four through six should enhance specific academic skills as well as independence and self-discipline.

At all levels, homework should be designed to promote personal interest in learning and discovery.

II. Sandburg Homework Definition

Homework is any mental activity, creative, technical, or aesthetic, accomplished outside of the classroom environment, that improves a child's understanding and ability to function successfully within the world.

III. Homework Structure

A. Homework is most effective when assigned on a regular basis, and students in all grades are required to spend a weekly minimum amount of time on homework activities.

A homework policy based on time requirements permits flexibility. Families can plan ahead and coordinate homework times with other activities. For example, a fifth grader with a heavy baseball schedule can arrange both homework time and baseball practice with some advance planning. On practice days, homework sessions might be scheduled after school, before dinner, after dinner, or students might choose to double up on the week days that are not filled with extra activities. The key is knowing in advance that assignments and specified amounts of time are required for schoolwork and then scheduling both homework and family activities on the family calendar.

B. In order to develop positive study habits, a daily, long-range developmental progression is most effective. Sandburg families are asked to support the following minimum time requirements.

Kindergarten	10 minutes, 4 times per week
1st Grade	15-20 minutes, 4 times per week
2nd Grade	15-20 minutes, 4 times per week
3rd Grade	30 minutes, 4 times per week
4th Grade	30-45 minutes, 4 times per week
5th Grade	50 minutes, 4 times per week
6th Grade	60 minutes, 4 times per week

C. Required Work: In order to foster motivation and effective study habits, a mix of mandatory, teacher-assigned homework and student-choice projects are required of every student.

Each teacher will assign work that is deemed valuable for the growth of his/her students. Students are required to complete mandatory work (teacher-assigned) and, in addition, to choose personally meaningful work to fill remaining time requirements. Students are encouraged to pursue their own interests through self-choice projects. Individual choice, within guidelines set by their individual teachers, will promote the completion of work that has personal meaning for the student. A mix of teacher-assigned, mandatory homework and self-choice projects promotes student responsibility and independence and will also promote increased amounts of time devoted to homework. Both teacher professionalism and unique family values are supported.

Teachers will not be asked to prescribe additional individual assignments for each student in order to meet time requirements. However, when deemed necessary, teachers or families may request remedial or individualized homework for practice of academic skills.

D. Suggested Supplemental/Self-Choice Activities. By focusing on the amount of time spent, this homework system promotes individual effort rather than competition with other students. All students will be completing teacher assignments and sometimes individual assignments. All students will have a minimum amount of time to spend doing homework each week.

Many students will find that they finish teacher-assigned work before the end of the week and are left with extra time. They must then decide how to spend that time; the ultimate responsibility is to their own emerging awareness of themselves as scholars.

Your child's teacher will make suggestions for supplemental activities. Some will use these suggestions, others will pursue their own paths of interest. For example, one child may choose to write letters, others may use their time to finish a story, complete an art project, design a science experiment, learn the multiplication tables, or build a rocket. Reading is a high priority for filling required self-choice time. The books your child chooses to read will be a result of the literature read in class and the student's own interest in themes, authors, or genres. Your classroom teacher will send home a classroom policy which will indicate acceptable student homework activities.

Below are some of the Sandburg survey self-choice activities suggested by parents and teachers:

- Art: lessons, exhibits, museums
- Community: environmental activities, tutoring, senior citizens volunteer
- Computer: keyboard practice, computer-aided design, geography games, etc.
- Current Events: reports, discussion, writing editorials
- Hobbies: Chess clubs, rocket building, map making, story-telling, dramatics
- Home Projects: measuring (primary age-level cooking activities)
- Languages: classes, studying language tapes
- Math: puzzles, practical problems, fact practice
- Music: band activities, composing, attending symphonies, performances
- Reading: fiction or nonfiction, alone or with an adult or sibling
- Science: experiments and projects, Science Center trips, science exhibits, science demonstrations, classes
- Writing: letters, diaries, reports, creative writing

Note: The above list is not meant to be exhaustive nor are these learning activities to be used as substitutes for mandatory, teacher-assigned projects. They are to be used to fulfill time requirements not already taken up by teacher assignments, and to promote individual interests and independence. In this way, both teacher professionalism and unique family values are supported.

For Students: A helpful basic guideline for choosing a self-directed project and deciding if the project fits the Sandburg definition of homework is: first, ask yourself, "What will I learn from this?" Then be prepared to answer your parent's and/or teacher's query: "What will you learn by doing this project?" Your answer will help your teacher decide whether the activity counts as homework.

E. Accountability:

TEACHERS

. . . will provide a weekly Homework Form for their students, with the exception of Sandburg Kindergarten teachers who will provide a monthly schedule. The homework form will have spaces for teacher-assigned work and for student-chosen projects. Teacher priorities are valued; assigned homework will vary among individual teachers based on their judgement as to what is important for their students. The addition of self-choice types of assignments eliminates the need for make-work assignments to satisfy time requirements. Required self-choice assignments promote work that has personal meaning for each student.

Both types of assignments (teacher-assigned and student-chosen) are required. However, some students may use all of their required time finishing teacher-assigned work or exploring an assignment in greater depth. Other students may finish teacher-assigned work relatively quickly and will use the remainder of their time developing their interests by choosing individual projects.

Teacher assignments will be written on the homework schedule either by the student or by the classroom teacher depending upon the student's grade-level.

Homework policies for each class, grades one though six, will be collected in a Homework Notebook and will be available upon request at the central office for interested parents and teachers.

A recording system will be used in order to alert parents and students on a weekly basis as to whether or not homework was completed. Each classroom teacher will provide a description of their recording system for students and parents. The goal of each classroom recording system is to promote increased student accountability and to provide timely feedback to families concerning their child's study habits.

STUDENTS

. . . are responsible for daily recording of time and homework activities on their homework schedule. Students in grades three through six will be required to keep their homework calendars in a three ring binder (no Trapper Keepers or Peechees please). Students return the homework schedule to the classroom on a weekly basis.

Students are required to complete teacher-assigned projects and to choose projects to fulfill time requirements not already filled by teacher assignments.

Student self-recording is a valuable teaching tool and a factor in self-motivation and independence. At the kindergarten and primary level, parents can support their students by taking dictation (helping their child record homework projects and the amount of time spent).

PARENTS OR CAREGIVERS

. . . are asked to monitor their children's homework time in order to assure that the required amount of time is spent. Parents indicate by initialling or signing the homework schedule that times indicated have been spent.

Parents are asked to promote the completion of homework by requiring a routine time to be set aside for homework and to encourage effort by praising their student for time on task and concentrated effort, showing interest in learning projects, and providing help when necessary or when their student shows signs of frustration.

Because assignments and minimum time requirements are clearly specified, arguments about homework are reduced. (Parent to Son or Daughter: "You are finished with your teacher's assignment? Great! Now what are you going to choose to do with the time you have left?")

The Parent Refrain: "Everybody's Doing It"
(Spending Time Doing Homework)

F. Evaluation and Feedback. Grading of homework is not always deemed necessary, especially at primary grade levels (kindergarten through third). However, homework is most effective when commented upon and when completion is noted. At older grade levels grading can be effective, especially when accompanied by specific suggestions for tackling the next learning step. At the beginning of the school year your child's teacher will provide guidelines as to what and how assignments are to be graded.

Most teacher-assigned homework will be assessed in some way, with comments or grades and credit for completion. Self-choice work will fulfill remaining time requirements and also be given credit for completion. The effect of homework completion will be reflected in overall achievement in subject areas and in the development of study skills. Self-choice projects provide a rich source of information about individual students' interests and strengths.

A homework evaluation will indicate whether or not students are completing homework time requirements. The specific form of this evaluation will be determined by your child's teacher. The homework evaluation will reflect effort expended to meet time requirements. Homework quality will also be reflected in academic achievement (writing, reading, math, social studies, etc.).

G. Routine. A homework system encompassing grades kindergarten through six that is a routine part of learning and everyday life will build independent study habits and reinforce effort. Consistent parental support for routine daily study (Monday through Thursday) is necessary in order to support our children's academic growth. Student self-recording of activities and time spent on homework will help build effective habits.

H. Capsule Comments:

1. Homework schedules go home on Monday (or the first school day of the week). Kindergarten schedules go home on the first school day of the month. Teacher assignments will not always appear on Monday. Teacher assignment days will vary depending on the learning requirements of the class or the individual. Older students will be expected to write assignment dates on their calendars.

2. Required homework is listed on the schedule. (By the teacher or by the student depending upon grade level and classroom)

3. Students are to spend a minimum of ________* minutes a day every week on homework. (*See time requirements for your child's grade level.)

4. Work completed and time spent are to be indicated in the spaces provided on the weekly schedule. For example, to indicate reading as homework, indicate the book title and number of pages read.

5. Parents, please sign the schedule before homework is returned. This is an important part of our communication network.

6. Completed homework (neatly done!) will usually be due on Friday or the last day of the school week. Some assignments may be long-range.

7. Homework will be evaluated by each classroom teacher. The assessment and evaluation system will be com-

municated to parents at the beginning of the school year. The goal of the evaluation system will be to recognize and reward effort.

IV. Homework Committee Support

Future activities, based on parent and teacher collaboration, are:

1. Prepare information for parents with ideas and suggestions for providing an environment that supports conflict-free homework and a love of learning.

2. Communicate the results of the Sandburg homework surveys and provide summaries of research gathered by the homework committee.

3. Develop a homework support system for Sandburg students and parents. Homework assistance programs are in the planning stages and will be designed for those children and parents who request support.

4. Conduct an ongoing review of the homework system in order to respond to unanticipated problems, to make improvements, and to insure that problem areas do not undermine the entire system. ("Fine tuning" on a regular basis.)

We believe that a student starting out in kindergarten in 1992-1993 at Sandburg and living with this system will be well served. The developmental homework structure described above can act as a scaffold. Our children use it to develop discipline and self-esteem until the exterior support is no longer needed. By sixth grade we expect these students to be self-motivated and thus accomplish home learning without undue prompting or nagging. Study will simply have become a satisfying way of life.

SANDBURG TEACHERS AND PARENTS

Sandburg Homework Committee

Chairman: Chris Larson

Staff Representative: Barb Woolsey

Teachers:	*Parents:*
Nadia Armstrong	Sue Faulds
Nancy Mendenhall	Joy Hagen
Eileen McMackin	Rob McCauley
Barb Roesgen	Kay Morison
Heidi Yamamoto	Stathis Papanicolaou
	Richard Pierce
	Bill Smith
	Liz Wattula

APPENDIX C

SANDBURG FOLLOW-UP SURVEY

Carl Sandburg '92-'93 Homework Policy Follow-up Questionnaire

(Parents, please circle your responses below. Please print written responses)

1. Grade level of your child (please complete one survey per child).

A. ___________

2. Are you familiar with Sandburg's new Homework Policy for the '92-'93 school year?

A. Yes   B. No

3. Has your child's teacher implemented a process to verify homework completion on a weekly basis?

A. Yes   B. No

4. Are you helping your K-3 grader record homework activity? Or . . . does your 4th-6th grader regularly record homework activity on their own?

A. Yes   B. No

5. Do you feel the new homework policy is more effective than the previous policy in generating:

Student Involvement?	A. Yes	B. No
Teacher Involvement?	A. Yes	B. No
Parent Involvement?	A. Yes	B. No

6. Do you see this new approach improving your child's attitude toward homework?

A. Yes   B. No

7. Do you feel the new policy effectively makes the student more responsible for their homework?

A. Yes   B. No

8. What improvements would you like to see in the Homework Policy?

A.______________________________

B.______________________________

C.______________________________

Sandburg Follow-Up Survey Results

350 families participated in the follow-up survey. The results are summarized as follows:

100 percent of the parent respondents indicated that they were familiar with the new policy.

Ninety percent of the teachers had implemented a process to verify homework.

Eighty-five percent of the parents indicated that their children were recording their homework times.

Eighty-three percent indicated that the homework policy is more effective in generating student involvement.

Seventy-five percent indicated that the new policy is more effective in generating teacher involvement.

Eighty-two percent indicated that the homework policy was more effective in generating parent involvement.

Seventy-two percent indicated the new approach improved their child's attitude towards homework.

Eighty-four percent indicated the students were becoming more responsible for handing in homework.

The results reported above included data from classrooms in which the new policy was not in place. In these classrooms students were not required to record the number of minutes spent, nor were they required to use a weekly homework accountability system. The homework systems in these classrooms did not generate as much student and parent involvement, increased responsibility for completing homework, or increase in positive attitudes. The community reception for the homework system was overall hearty acceptance.

Appendix D

Charlie Lake Homework Summary

Study skills have been called the "invisible curriculum." Information and strategies offered in this handout will improve homework and study skills of all students.

Why do teachers assign homework?

Teachers assign homework for several reasons:

1. Homework develops lifelong learning habits.
2. Homework provides time for practicing class learning and for preparing upcoming lessons.
3. Homework teaches students to work independently, to develop self-discipline, and to establish and value effort.
4. Homework provides opportunity for parents to motivate and to encourage their children's school success.
5. It is known to have a powerful effect on school achievement and study habits.
6. Homework research over the last twenty years indicate that homework should be assigned at all grade levels. A mixture of both mandatory and self-choice is most beneficial to students.

What is the goal underlying the Charlie Lake Homework System?

To establish study habits that enable our children to become life-long learners.

What message is sent to our children through this system?

Here is a way to be responsible for your own learning. You are capable of making choices that enhance your unique abilities.

Why do so many parents like this system?

1. Arguing about homework is reduced; expectations are clear.
2. Homework becomes a self-directed habit.
3. A channel for weekly communication about academic matters is maintained with the classroom teacher.
4. Family priorities are valued. There is built-in flexibility to accommodate family schedules.
5. Meaningful work is accomplished.

Why do teachers like this system?

1. Teacher priorities are valued; assigned homework will vary among individual teachers based on their judgments as to what is important for their students. No "make-work" to satisfy arbitrary homework requirements.

2. Responsibility is placed where it belongs: with the student.
3. The system is easy to monitor and evaluate.
4. Communication with the home is maintained with a minimum of time and effort. It creates a partnership between the school and its families.
5. Meaningful work is accomplished.
6. Daily homework is known to result in larger positive effects than homework required less often.

Why do students respond to this system?

1. Choices and interests are recognized and valued.
2. Expectations are clear.
3. Meaningful work is accomplished.

How does the Charlie Lake Homework System work?

PRIMARY (YEAR 2 – YEAR 4, OR GRADES 1–3)

Primary students usually have a positive attitude toward homework. Homework is given to foster success experiences and to enhance love of learning. It also helps to develop students' sense of responsibility and establishes the value of effort. Parents have the opportunity to praise and encourage efforts and to influence their children by the value they place on education. A habitual means of communication between the teacher and home is established.

Students in the primary years will frequently be asked to take books home for home reading to parents or siblings. They will benefit greatly from being read to on a regular basis. Some primary students will be taking home a response journal or "Back and Forth Book" and inviting your comments and responses on a regular basis. At times, students will take assignments home to provide them with extra skill practice. Parental help will be enlisted in promoting student accountability. Your child's teacher will be communicating the homework routines for the 1993-1994 school year in the near future.

INTERMEDIATE (L1 – L4 OR GRADES 4 – 7)

1. Homework sheets go home on Monday or the first school day of the week.
2. Required homework is listed on the schedule.
3. Students are to spend a minimum of __________ minutes a day or ______ hours per week on homework. (See time guidelines following these suggestions.)
4. Work completed and time spent are to be filled in daily in the space provided on the schedule. To indicate reading as homework, indicate the title and number of pages read.
5. Parents are asked to please sign the schedule before homework is returned.

6 Completed homework (neatly done!) is due on Friday or the last day of the school week.

7. Teacher input and student self-evaluation will be the basis for anecdotal remarks which will assess and evaluate the homework assignments. Criteria for evaluation will include:

- satisfactory completion
- time requirements met
- additional time spent
- personal choices made.

8. Examples of suggested self-choice activities which fulfill time requirements:

- Reading a book (silently or aloud to another family member)
- Discussion creative writing assignments
- Writing a letter
- Practicing automatic recall of basic math facts
- Playing math games, scrabble, etc.
- Practicing a musical instrument
- Music Lessons
- Watching a National Geographic program on television or video
- Teaching family members a song or dance learned at school

- Working on a social studies or science project
- Building a model
- Doing a science project
- Working in a "challenge book"
- Preparing interviews
- Taking part in a "family togetherness" activity
- Attending a play or other activity at the cultural center
- Practicing calligraphy
- Reading an origami book and making some projects

Your child's teacher may have other examples. You may come up with many more. Talk with the teacher if you have any questions or suggestions.

Suggested Daily Minimums: Monday-Thursday

Entry level: 10-15 minutes per night (reading to your child or talking about his or her school experiences.)

P2 (Gr.1): 20 minutes (80 minutes per week)
P3 (Gr.2): 25 minutes (100 minutes per week)
P4 (Gr.3): 30 minutes (2 hours per week)
L1 (Gr.4): 40 minutes (160 minutes per week)
L2 (Gr.5): 50 minutes (200 minutes per week)
L3 (Gr.6): 60 minutes (4 hours per week)
L4 (Gr.7): 70 minutes (280 minutes per week)

Note: Time guidelines were modified for the 1993-94 school year in response to parent feedback.

Monitoring the time spent on homework provides a way parents can support the classroom teacher. There should be minimal parent involvement in the intermediate levels. The parents' job is to praise efforts, monitor the time spent, and to initial the homework sheet. Don't do the homework! This is the student's work! This is not the parents' time to teach.

By attending to both assigned and self-selected work, we can, as a collaborative team of parents, teachers and administrators, help our children develop the study habits and positive attitudes that enable them to become effective life-long learners.

Bibliography

Baumrind, D. (1977). Socialization determinants of personal agency. *Paper presented at the biennial meetings of the Society for Research in Child Development*, New Orleans.

Bloom, B. S. (1984). The search for methods of group instruction as effective as one-to-one tutoring. *Educational Leadership*, 4(8),4-17.

Brady, S. & Jacobs, S. (1994). *Mindful of Others.* Portsmouth, NH: Heinemann Press.

Cantor, L., & Hausner, L. (1987). *Homework Without Tears.* New York: Harper & Row.

Caplan, N., Choy, M., & Whitmore, J. (1992, February). Indochinese refugee families and academic achievement. *Scientific American*, pp. 36-42.

Chall, J., Jacobs, V., & Baldwin, L. (1990). *Why poor children fall behind.* Cambridge, MA: Harvard University Press.

Chavkin, C. (1989). Debunking the myth about minority parents. *Educational Horizons*, pp. 119-123.

Chubb, J.E. (1988). Why the current wave of school reform will fail. *The Public Interest*, pp.28-49.

Chen, C., Stevenson, H. (1989). Homework: A cross-cultural examination. *Child Development*, *60*, 551-561.

Coleman, J. S., Hoffer, T., & Kilgore, S. (1982). *High School achievement: Public, Catholic and private schools compared.* New York: Basic Books.

Cooper, H. M. (1989). Synthesis of research on homework. *Educational Research, 47*, 85-91.

Cooper, H. M. (1991). *Homework* (Research on Teaching Monograph Series). White Plains, NY: Longman Inc.

Dweck, C. S. (1986). Motivational processes affecting learning. *American Psychologist, 41*.

Easton, J., & Bennett, A. (1990). *Achievement effects of homework in sixth grade classrooms*. Boston, MA: American Educational Research Association. (Eric Document Reproduction Service No. ED 320 675).

Epstein, J. L. (1983). *Homework practices, achievements, and behaviors of elementary school students.* Baltimore, MD: Johns Hopkins University. (ERIC Document Reproduction Service No. Ed 250 351).

England, D. A., & Flatly, J. K. (1985). Homework–and why. *Phi Delta Kappa*, pp. 11-12.

Featherstone, H. (1985). Homework. *The Harvard Education Letter, 1*, 1.

Fish, M. C., & Mendola, L. R. (1986). The effect of self-instruction training on homework completion in an elementary special education classroom. *School Psychology Review, 15*, 268-276.

Foyle, H. C. (1984). *The effects of preparation and practice homework on student achievement in tenth-grade American History.* Unpublished doctoral dissertation, Kansas State University, Manhattan, KS.

Foyle, H. C., & Bailey, G. D. (1985). *Homework in the classroom: Can it make a difference in student achievement?* Paper presented at the annual meeting of the Association for Supervision and Curriculum Development, Chicago. (ERIC Document Reproduction Service No. ED 257 796).

Frederick, W. C., & Walberg, H. J. (1980). Learning as a function of time. *Journal of Educational Research, 73*, 183-194.

Freisen, C. D. (1978). *The results of surveys, questionnaires, and polls regarding homework.* (ERIC Document Reproduction Service No. ED 159 174).

Freisen, C. D. (1979). *The results of homework versus no-homework research studies.* (ERIC Document Reproduction Service No. ED 167 508).

Gettinger, M. (1984). Achievement as a function of time spent in learning and time needed for learning. *American Educational Research Journal, 21*, 617-628.

Green, A. & Stedman, H. (1993). *Education provision, educational attainment and the needs of industry.* London: National Institution of Economic and Social Research.

Hamburg, D. (1992). Speech to the United States Congress: television violence. *Congressional Record,* July 27.

Henderson, V. L., & Dweck, C. S. (1990). Motivation and achievement. In S. S. Feldman and G. R. Elliot (Eds.), *At the Threshold: the Developing Adolescent.* Cambridge, MA: Harvard University Press.

John-Steiner, V. (1985). Notebooks of the mind. Albuquerque: University of New Mexico Press.

Keith, T., Reimers, T., Fehrman, P., Pottembaum, S., & Aubey, L. (1986). Parental involvement, homework, and TV time: Direct and indirect effects on high school involvement. *Journal of Educational Psychology, 78*, 373-380.

Keith, T. Z. (1987). Children and homework. In A. Thomas & J. Grimes (Eds.), *Children's needs: Psychological perspectives* (pp. 275-282). Washington, DC: National Association of School Psychologists.

Keith, T. Z. (1986). Homework. *Kappa Delta Pi*, pp. 9-12.

Keith, T. Z. (1982). Time spent on homework and high school grades: A large-sample path analysis. *Journal of educational psychology, 74*, 248-253.

Keith, T. Z., & Page, E. B. (1985). Homework works at school: National evidence for policy changes. *School Psychology Review, 14*, 351-359.

LaConte, R. T. (1981). Homework as a learning experience: *What research says to the teacher. (ERIC Document Reproduction Service No. ED 217 022).*

Levine, V., & Worley, W. R. (1985). *The impact of television and homework time on cognitive and noncognitive outcomes.* Paper presented at the meeting of the American Educational Research Association, Chicago, IL.

Mackenzie, D. E. (1983). Research for school improvement: An appraisal of some recent trends. *Educational Researcher, 12*, 5-17.

Majoribanks, K. (1983). The evaluation of a family learning model.Studies *in Educational Evaluation, 9*, 343-357.

Matthews, J. (1993, March 1). Psst Kid, Wanna buy a . . . used math book? *Newsweek*, pp. 62-63.

Merrow, J. (1985). Children and television; Natural parents. *Phi Delta Kappa*, 67, 211-214.

Montemayer, R. (1990). Parents and adolescents in conflict. In R. Muss (Ed.), *Adolescent Behavior and Society.* New York: McGraw-Hill.

Murphy, J., & Decker, K. (1990). Homework use at the high school level: Implications for Principals. *NASSP Bulletin, 74*,40-43.

Muss, R. E. (1990). Adolescent behavior and society. New York: McGraw-Hill.

National Commission on Excellence in Education (1983). *A Nation at Risk: The Imperative for Educational Reform.* Washington, DC: United States Department of Education.

Oakes, J. (1985). *Keeping Track.* Yale University Press, New Haven, Conn.

Palardy, J. M. (1988). The effect of homework policies on student achievement. *NASSP Bulletin, 72*(507), 14-17.

Paschal, R. A., Weinstein, T., & Walberg, H. J. (1984). The effects of homework on learning: A quantitative synthesis. *Journal of Educational Research, 78*(2), 97-104.

Pendergrass, R. A. (1985). Homework; Is it really a basic? *Clearinghouse, 58*(7), 310-314.

Pickens, I., & Kies, A. (1988). *Knock out academic stress via leisure reading*. (ERIC Document Reproduction Service No. ED 386 996).

Quackenbush, R., & Gastineau, J. (1989). The *academic skills workshop: A parent-child group intervention to stop school failure.* (ERIC Document Reproduction Service No. ED 318 961).

Ross, P., Project Director (1993). *National excellence: A case for developing America's talent.* Office of Educational Research and Improvement, U.S. Department of Education.

Seginer, R. (1983). Parent's educational expectations and children's academic achievement: A literature review. *Merrill Palmer Quarterly, 29*, 1-23.

Stevenson, H., Chen, C., & Lee, S. (1992). Mathematics achievement of Chinese, Japanese, and American children: Ten years later. *Science*, *259*, 53-58.

Stevenson, H., Lee, S.Y., & Stigler, J. W. (1986). Mathematics achievement of Chinese, Japanese, and American children.*Science*, 231, 693-699.

Stanley, J. C. (1980). Manipulate important educational variables.*Educational Psychologist, 15,* 164-171.

Turvey, J. (1986). Homework-Its importance to student achievement. *NASSP Bulletin, 70*, 27-35.

Walberg, H. J. (1984). Improving the productivity of America's schools. *Educational Leadership, 41*(8), 19-30.

Walberg, H. J., & Shanahan, T. (1983). High school effects on individual students. *Educational Researcher, 12*(7), 4-9.

Walberg, H. J., Paschal, R. A., & Weinstein, T. (1985). Homework's powerful effect on learning. *Educational Leadership, 42*(7), 76-79.

Williams, P. A., Haertel, E. H., Haertel, G. D., & Walberg, H. J. (1982). The impact of leisure-time television on school learning. *American Educational Research Journal, 19*, 19-50.

Wolf, R. M. (1979). Achievement in the United States. In H. J. Walberg (Ed.), *Educational environments and effects*. CA: McCutcheon.